Animal Testing

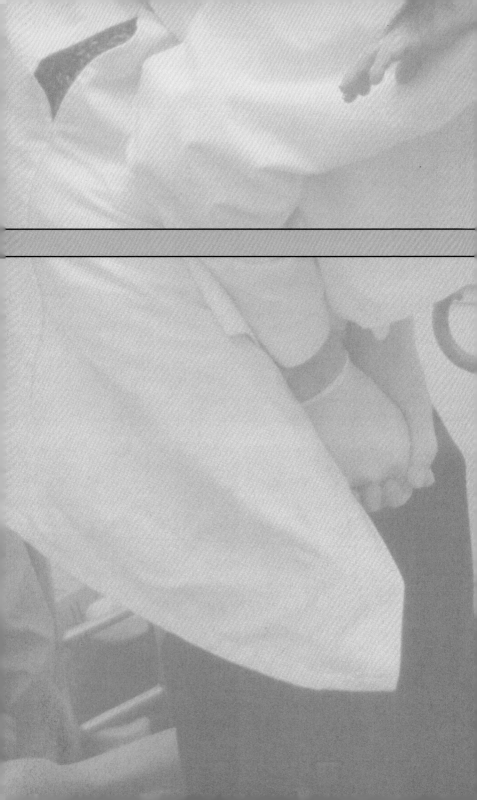

Open for Debate

Animal Testing

Karen Judson

mc **Marshall Cavendish**
Benchmark
New York

*With special thanks to Dr. Greg Popken,
Division of Pediatric Endocrinology,
University of North Carolina at Chapel Hill,
for his expert review of this manuscript.*

Marshall Cavendish Benchmark
Marshall Cavendish
99 White Plains Road
Tarrytown, NY 10591
www.marshallcavendish.us

All Internet sites were available and accurate when sent to press.

Library of Congress Cataloging-in-Publication Data
Judson, Karen, 1941-
Animal testing / by Karen Judson.
p. cm. — (Open for debate)
Includes bibliographical references and index.

ISBN 0-7614-1882-2

1. Animal experimentation—Juvenile literature. 2. Animal
experimentation—Moral and ethical aspects—Juvenile literature.
3. Animal rights—Juvenile literature. I. Title. II. Series.
HV4915.J83 2005
179'.4—dc22
2004021815

Photo research by Linda Sykes Picture Research, Inc., Hilton Head, SC

Corbis/Robert Maas: cover

Corbis-Sygma/Paliava Bagla: 6; Bettmann/Corbis: 16, 18, 23, 100; Corbis: 25, 45; Getty Images/Paul
Harris: 43; Corbis/Dan Lamont: 50; Photo Researchers, Inc./PHANIE: 54; Corbis/Charles Rotkin: 61, 75;
Corbis-Sygma/Touhig Sion: 65, 94; Corbis/Hulton Deutsch: 69; Corbis/Richard Nowitz: 81; Corbis/Douglas
Kirkland: 86; Photo Researchers, Inc./James King-Holmes: 111; Photo Researchers, Inc.: 113.

Printed in China

135642

Contents

A SCIENTIST IN A RESEARCH LABORATORY IN NEW DELHI, INDIA, IS SHOWN WITH CAGED RABBITS USED FOR DRUG TESTING AND BIOMEDICAL RESEARCH.

Do you remember the vaccinations you received when you were a small child? Most kids hate shots, but these vaccinations are intended to protect children from serious diseases that can affect them for the rest of their lives, or even kill them. The vaccinations are also given for public health reasons. To prevent communicable diseases from spreading throughout the population, all states now require proof of immunization or other evidence of immunity against some of these diseases in order for children to be admitted to school. The requirements vary from state to state, however, and exemptions may be granted for medical, moral, or religious reasons.

Before these vaccines were available, parents in the United States could expect that every year:

- **Polio would paralyze 10,000 children.**

- **Rubella (German measles) would infect as many as 20,000 newborns and some would suffer birth defects and mental retardation.**

- **Measles would infect about 4 million children, killing 3,000.**

- **Diphtheria would be a common cause of death in schoolchildren.**

- **A bacterium called Haemophilus influenzae type b (Hib) would cause meningitis (an infection of the tissue covering the brain or spinal cord) in 15,000 children. Many infected children who survived would be brain-damaged.**

- **Pertussis (whooping cough) would kill thousands of infants.**

The Childhood Vaccination Series

For children born in the United States, the following vaccinations are recommended (some are required to enter school) by the American Academy of Pediatrics, the American Academy of Family Practice, and the Advisory Committee on Immunization Practices of the United States Centers for Disease Control and Prevention (CDC):

• **Hepatitis B (HepB or HBV):** Four doses as follows: the first soon after birth; the second at one month of age; the third at four months of age; and the fourth at six to eighteen months of age.

• **Diphtheria, Tetanus (lock-jaw) and Pertussis (whooping cough) (DTP):** Five doses administered at two, four, and six months; at fifteen to eighteen months, and at four to six years. Tetanus/diphtheria booster at age eleven. Tetanus booster at ten-year intervals thereafter.

• **Haemophilus influenzae type b (Hib):** Administered at age four months, and again at two years.

• **Inactivated Polio:** Four doses at two months, four months, six to eighteen months, and four to six years.

• **Measles, mumps, and rubella (MMR):** Two doses, one administered at twelve to fifteen months, and the second at four to six years.

• **Varicella (chickenpox):** Administered during any doctor's visit at or after twelve to eighteen months of age.

• **Pneumococcal conjugatevaccine (PCV7):** To protect against pneumonia, blood infections and meningitis (a serious infection of the lining of the brain or spinal cord) caused by the pneumococcus bacterium. Four doses: at two, four, and six months of age. Another form of the vaccine is given to children age two and over whose immune systems are vulnerable.

• **Hepatitis A:** Administered to children and adolescents in selected states and regions, and to certain high-risk groups.

• **Influenza:** Administered annually to children age six to twenty-three months who have certain risk factors, such as asthma, heart disease, sickle cell disease, human immunodeficiency virus (HIV), diabetes, and others.

As scientists worked on developing vaccines for these diseases through the 1800s and 1900s, most historical accounts say that they used animals to test them. Monkeys were used in most cases, but mice and guinea pigs were also employed to develop the polio and diphtheria vaccines, respectively.

Methods used to improve human health often involve animal testing. Animals are used as surrogates (substitutes) for people for three main purposes: to test drugs, vaccines, and consumer products; for biomedical research; and for education. The use of animals for these purposes has become a hotly debated topic in the United States and in Europe, where many protest the practice of using animals for experimentation and testing.

Early animal researchers were often inhumane, in part because:

1. **Early scientists knew little about animal nervous systems, and many believed nonhuman animals were incapable of feeling pain.**

2. **Judeo-Christian religions taught that God had given people "dominion" over animals.**

3. **Anesthetics were not available before the mid-1800s.**

It is also true, however, that scientific methods have improved considerably over time, and that attitudes within the scientific community toward animals used in research have generally changed in that reputable scientists no longer treat animals inhumanely, or believe in a God-given right to use them to benefit people. In addition, groups opposing the cruel treatment of animals were influential in getting regulations passed to protect the welfare of animals.

The controversy over animal testing is not going to go away soon, however, because humans will continue to be plagued with dangerous new diseases and will continue to be exposed to new chemicals. And most members of the scientific community say that animal testing is still the most reliable way to learn how to protect people from these threats.

Globalization is partly responsible for the concern over the spread of new diseases. People need passports or visas to pass over national borders, but national borders do not stop the spread of disease. The United States has nearly 300 million people; world population stands at over six billion. Many people now travel the globe for business and pleasure. This has meant that diseases and disease environments have been imported to the United States from other countries and exported from the United State to countries abroad. For example, new diseases found for the first time in the United States within the last decade or two, such as the human immunodeficiency virus (HIV) and acquired immunodeficiency syndrome (AIDS), West Nile fever, monkey pox, severe acute respiratory syndrome (SARS), and Ebola, are proof that when human or animal vectors (carriers of disease organisms) cross national borders, so do diseases.

Smallpox vaccine, dating back to Edward Jenner's successful work in 1796 using the cowpox virus to develop a vaccination for smallpox, has recently helped people infected with monkey pox that was probably contracted from handling imported rats and prairie dogs.

Scientists continue to research a vaccine and possible cures for HIV/AIDS using animals as scientific models, and research is also under way to find vaccines for West Nile fever, SARS, and Ebola. A vaccine for the West Nile virus has been developed for horses, and scientists working with mice reported in 2003 that progress had been made that could lead to a human vaccine. Furthermore, in June 2004, scientists in London reported that an experimental vaccine for SARS sprayed into the nose protected African green monkeys against the SARS virus and could be developed to immunize humans against the disease.

Some people hate the idea that animals are used in scientific research and testing, because most people like animals and many keep them as pets, but the issue is complicated. Some people, including some scientists, object to the practice strictly on ethical and moral grounds, refuting or rejecting any scientific evidence that animal testing is helpful to humans. Others, also including many scientists, believe that historical accounts of cures and vaccines credited to animal testing and experimentation are not accurate, and that in today's world animal testing is outdated and, therefore, of little or no benefit. Another viewpoint many people hold is that even though animals are often killed as a necessary step in testing or biomedical experiments, the benefits to humans outweigh the reluctance many feel to use animals in this manner. Most people who are concerned with animal welfare, including the majority of researchers who use animals in their work, do not want animals to suffer unnecessarily. Moreover, animal welfare laws and the fact that good science requires conscientious treatment of research animals also contribute to the humane treatment of animals used as test subjects.

This text encourages you to make an *informed* decision about where you stand on the issue. Consider the scientific argument that says animal testing is necessary for human health and possibly even for human survival, as well as the arguments against animal testing that say animals have the right to live their lives in peace, without human use and exploitation. In addition, consider the argument that animal testing has outlived its usefulness. After you have considered evidence on all sides of the argument, use your critical thinking skills to decide where you stand on the controversial issue of animal testing.

How and When
It All Began

Animal testing and experimentation—using animals in place of humans in toxicity tests, experiments, and education—has a long history, both in Europe and the United States. It started centuries ago, primarily for two reasons:

• **Curiosity. Even in the Stone Age, when people cut into an animal they were probably curious about the various blood vessels and organs that were visible inside the creature's body.**

• **Convenience. Live humans were not generally available or willing to be operated on to satisfy another person's curiosity. Animals were the alternative. Early scientists cut into living and dead animals, as well as human corpses, to learn about the internal construction and function of bodily systems.**

Animal experimentation became the primary method of learning about anatomy, physiology, and disease processes because the state-supported Roman Catholic Church in early Greece and Rome forbade the dissection of human corpses. Church law was followed throughout Europe, and the church could charge an offender with heresy (ignoring or disagreeing with Church teachings), which was punishable by death. Curious physicians and other scientists, however, could cut into animals without danger to their lives or souls, because animals were said to have no souls. Some people believed that the absence of a soul also meant that nonhuman animals felt no pain.

Galen of Pergamon, physician to the gladiators in second century Rome and to the son of Roman ruler Marcus Aurelius, was an early scientist who was in the perfect position to study human anatomy. However, he could not explore deeply enough into the inner workings of the human body, because of the Church's prohibition against human dissection. Instead, he experimented on pigs, dogs, monkeys, and other animals. He assumed that biological systems and functions would be much the same throughout the animal kingdom, and he was one of the first early scientists to transfer his observations of animals to humans.

Galen's theory of health and disease was that the human body consisted of four "humors"—blood, phlegm, yellow bile, and black bile—and that when these substances were out of balance or when they otherwise malfunctioned, a person became ill. Although Galen was mistaken, his theories persisted for nearly 1,500 years. His theories persisted for so long because the Church continued to forbid dissecting human corpses, and because people failed to actively research physiology using animals. Galen's flawed "humors" theory influenced generations of physicians who came after him. (Bloodletting—opening a vein to drain blood from the body—was a common medical treatment well into the nineteenth century.)

During the seventeenth, eighteenth, and nineteenth centuries, many physicians, physiologists, naturalists, and other scientists studied anatomy, physiology, and disease processes by dissecting human corpses. They did so in secret at first because the Church continued to disapprove of human dissection. Some scientists paid grave robbers to provide corpses. The Church finally eased restrictions, and dissecting human corpses gained acceptance within scientific circles. It eventually became routine in medical schools because dissecting a human corpse was the most accurate way for students to learn anatomy.

Human dissection allowed students to replace Galen's antiquated theories of bodily humors with accurate theories of blood circulation, organ structure and function, and muscles and tendons and their relationship to bones. Moreover, human dissection was supplemented with animal studies, which could now be directed toward more specific ends. Knowledge about the human body and disease processes increased greatly during this time.

In 1628, in a series of experiments conducted at the anatomy school in Padua, Italy, William Harvey, an English physician, demonstrated the circulation of blood using animals. He applied the explanation to humans, thus, among the scientific community, showing the value of vivisection for accurately illustrating physiology as well as anatomy. (Vivisection means "to cut into living tissue." The term came to be used to describe animal experimentation.) Questions so long unanswered about how we breathe, digest food, and perform other bodily functions could now be shown to have physiological answers because of vivisection. As a result of Harvey's work, many other scientists now saw the value in working with animals. Consequently, the rate of animal testing increased steadily through the seventeenth century and into the eighteenth and nineteenth centuries.

In 1865, a French physiologist named Claude Bernard

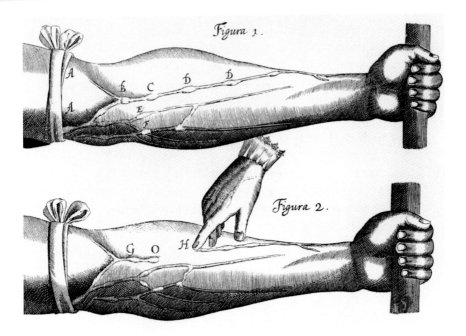

WILLIAM HARVEY WORKED WITH ANIMALS TO LEARN HOW BLOOD CIRCULATES THROUGH A LIVING SYSTEM.

published *Introduction to the Study of Experimental Medicine*. He had studied under Frenchman François Magendie, who was among the first to determine that bodily processes involved the co-functioning of several organs. Both scientists experimented extensively with animals, and in so doing became the target of critics of vivisection. In *Introduction to the Study of Experimental Medicine*, Bernard answered his critics:

> **Have we the right to make experiments on animals and vivisect them? . . . I think we have this right, wholly and absolutely. It would be strange indeed if we recognized man's right to make use of animals in every walk of life, for domestic service, for food,**

and then forbade him to make use of them for his own instruction in one of the sciences most useful to humanity. No hesitation is possible; the science of life can be established only through experiment, and we can save living beings from death only after sacrificing others. Experiments must be made either on man or on animals. Now I think that physicians already made too many dangerous experiments on man, before carefully studying them on animals. I do not admit that it is moral to try more or less dangerous or active remedies on patients in hospitals, without first experimenting with them on dogs; for I shall prove . . . that results obtained on animals may all be conclusive for man when we know how to experiment properly.

Bernard's theories were widely accepted among European scientists, and many more scientists became vivisectionists. Records kept in Great Britain of the numbers of research animals used in experiments each year show that the number of animal testing procedures increased from 311 in 1880 to over 95,000 in 1910. (Great Britain's 1876 Cruelty to Animals Act required English researchers to keep careful records of the numbers of research animals used in experiments each year, while the United States had no laws requiring that such numbers be recorded.)

Some vivisectionists believed that humans were justified in using animals for the benefit of people because people were so far above animals in every way that they should be able to use them at will. After all, the argument for vivisection often stated, aren't people the only animals capable of the depth of thought required for practicing scientific exploration, as well as ethical and moral behavior? And don't those qualities make people superior to animals?

A milestone in animal research was the development of

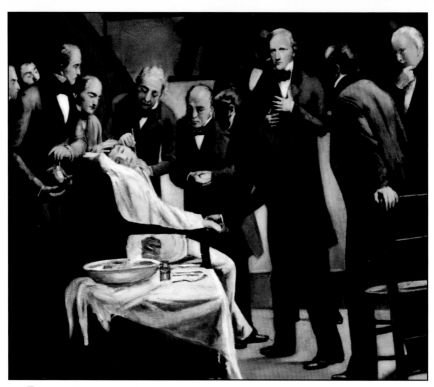

THE USE OF ETHER—AN ANESTHETIC—WAS A TREMENDOUS IMPROVEMENT IN SURGICAL TECHNIQUE, BOTH FOR PEOPLE BEING TREATED FOR MEDICAL CONDITIONS AND FOR ANIMALS USED IN RESEARCH.

ether, the first effective surgical anesthetic, credited to Crawford Long (1842) and William Morton (1846). (The two researchers did not work together.) After ether became available, scientists were able to use more sophisticated and humane surgical procedures in their work with animals.

Attitudes toward vivisection were greatly affected by Charles Darwin, a British naturalist, when he published his theory of evolution in *The Origin of Species by Means of Natural Selection* in 1859. Humans are not at the top of an evolutionary progression of animal species, Darwin concluded. They are simply a highly functioning species of animal that has survived through mutation and adaptation, and they are distantly related to all other animal species. Darwin's theory conflicted with various religious teachings, and many people disputed his theory. Over time, however, with the accumulation of fossil evidence to support it, Darwin's theory of evolution became widely accepted in scientific circles.

Darwin also influenced the acceptance of vivisection in that he supported animal research. "I know that physiology cannot possibly progress except by means of experiments on living animals," he once wrote in a letter, "and I feel with the deepest conviction that he who retards the progress of physiology commits a crime against mankind."

Another British naturalist, Thomas Huxley, expanded on Darwin's theory in 1863, when he claimed that people are more closely related to the apes—monkeys, gorillas, chimpanzees, and orangutans—than to any other species of animal. Darwin agreed with Huxley, and published his version of the kinship of people to apes in 1871 in *The Descent of Man*. Most people at that time considered humans superior to the rest of the animal kingdom, but the idea that humans had evolved from other life forms was a popular scientific conclusion.

The idea of human superiority over nonhuman animals was also grounded in Judeo-Christian religious teachings. In the early 1800s, the Bible, Genesis 1:26, was often quoted by vivisectionists and those who supported them. As paraphrased, the passage reads: "Let us make man to our image and likeness; and let him have dominion over the fishes of the sea, and the fowls of the air, and the beasts, and the whole earth, and every creeping creature that moveth upon the earth." Thus, the side chosen in the argument was often based on one's religious views, and whether it was morally right to consider humans above nonhuman animals, or to consider all living creatures as equal in the eyes of God.

Those people who saw animal testing as cruel, unethical, and unnecessary often did not believe that people should have "dominion" over animals and were generally influenced by the following:

- **Darwin's and Huxley's theories of humans' kinship with animals, especially primates (chimpanzees, gorillas, orangutans, baboons, and monkeys), increased the numbers of vivisectionists eager to find physiological similarities, and also the numbers of people who objected to vivisection.**

- **Scientists before the invention of anesthetics used crude methods that caused animals to suffer.**

- **Scientific progress was often slow, and results were not always dramatic enough to be widely publicized.**

- **It was difficult for scientists to defend the practice, because the general public had more sympathy with the plight of caged dogs, cats, and rabbits than with the confusing and sometimes arrogant explanations of scientists in white coats.**

Because many people did not want animals to be abused, groups concerned with animal welfare became active in Europe, especially in Great Britain. Anticruelty laws were passed in Great Britain first, in the early to mid-1800s, then in the United States in response to the animal welfare groups' insistence that the government act to prevent unnecessary cruelty to animals. Throughout the 1800s, animal welfare proponents in Great Britain and the United States urged their governments to protect animals by law—in methods of slaughter, treatment of farm and domestic animals, and in animal experimentation.

Early animal welfare groups called themselves antivivisectionists. Some members of these groups took a radical approach to opposing animal experimentation, demanding nothing less than an end to the practice. Those antivivisectionists who were more militant in their objections often threatened scientists and their families and destroyed property where scientific experiments were being conducted. The more radical antivivisectionist movement had not yet spread to America, but by the late 1800s, animal welfare groups were also becoming active in the United States. Clearly, anti-vivisectionist groups were splitting into two camps: those concerned with animal *welfare* and the humane treatment of animals, but not willing to commit crimes to defend their position, and those sometimes willing to commit illegal acts to draw attention to the *rights* of animals—humans and animals should have the same rights to coexist without cruelty, unnecessary pain, or exploitation.

The first animal welfare group in the United States was the American Society for the Prevention of Cruelty to Animals, founded by Henry Bergh in 1866. American Humane, also called the American Humane Association, an organization concerned with the welfare of children and animals, has existed since 1877. The Humane Society of the United States was founded in 1954 and, including affiliates, now has a membership estimated at from five to eight million.

The many animal welfare groups in Great Britain and later in the United States spurred the United States and Great Britain to pass laws concerned with animal welfare. Great Britain passed Martin's Act in 1822, which was intended to protect horses and cattle. In the United States, New York passed the first animal anticruelty law in 1829, prohibiting the malicious injuring or killing of farm animals such as horses, oxen, cattle, or sheep. By 1907 every American state had passed anticruelty acts, and by 1923 laws in most states also prohibited animal neglect and abandonment, cockfighting, and certain types of hunting traps.

In 1958, the U.S. Congress passed ·the Humane Methods of Slaughter Act. The act required slaughterhouses to stun animals before killing them, but applied only to meat sold to the federal government. The law eventually became the standard for all animals slaughtered for meat.

The Animal Welfare Act, passed in 1966, governs the handling of laboratory animals in the United States. It is discussed in detail in Chapter 2.

As scientific research progressed during the eighteenth and nineteenth centuries, so, too, did the methods used in animal experimentation. After the mid-1800s, anesthetics were used for painful procedures; consequently, fewer animal subjects were made to suffer in the name of science. Biomedical research laboratories became affiliated with hospitals, so that students could observe the disease process in humans and recognize similarities and differences that occurred in animal studies. Conscientious teachers also informed students that not all animal studies were accurate human models, and that animals used in studies should be treated humanely.

Some members of antivivisection groups, however, in both Europe and the United States, continued to believe that any use of animals in science was inhumane, unethical, and immoral. Animal rights groups, as the more militant animal welfare groups were called, targeted scientific research almost exclusively. Thus, groups that began as more moderate animal welfare organizations gave rise to radical groups that championed a complete bill of rights for animals, and used extreme tactics to get their messages across to politicians, research scientists, and the public.

Philosopher Peter Singer's book, *Animal Liberation: A New Ethics for Our Treatment of Animals,* published in 1975, marked the beginning of an organized animal rights movement in the United States. Singer pointed out that in addition to human beings, other conscious beings are capable of suffering and feeling happiness, so they should receive the same moral consideration and the same rights as humans. Singer claimed "speciesism"—discriminating against animals

A CARTOON BY THOMAS NAST, CALLED "THE DEFRAUDED GORILLA," SHOWS EVOLUTIONIST CHARLES DARWIN (LEFT), AND HENRY BERGH, FOUNDER OF THE ASPCA.

of nonhuman species—was just as undesirable in human society as sexism or racism. Singer called for the liberation of animals, based on equality of moral consideration and their capacity to suffer:

> **The fundamental common interest between humans and other animals remains the interest in not experiencing pain and suffering. The only acceptable limit to our moral concern is the point at which there is no awareness of pain or pleasure, and no preferences of any kind. That is why the principle of equal consideration of interests has implications for what we may do to rats, but not for what we may do to lettuces. Rats can feel pain, and pleasure. Lettuces can't.**

Animal rights groups in Great Britain and the United States continue to gain members and sponsorship, and many such groups hope to influence politicians to pass laws against all scientific research using animals. The membership of groups formed to oppose animal testing includes scientists, some of whom claim that animal experiments did not contribute to scientific knowledge in the past and cannot do so in the future. Many members of such groups have declared that they will never favor animal experimentation, even if it means that their own children could die of a disease because animal testing was not allowed in researching a vaccine or a cure.

Those who are in favor of animal testing point out all the benefits derived from the practice. For example, just as animal experimentation has benefited humans, it has also benefited pets and farm animals. In France in the 1800s, for instance, cholera had killed thousands of chickens when Louis Pasteur discovered that a weakened cholera broth injected into his hens left them immune to the dis-

LOUIS PASTEUR GREW THE RABIES VIRUS IN THE BRAINS AND SPINAL CORDS OF RABBITS.

ease (1879). Pasteur also discovered a vaccine for anthrax in farm animals (1881), and grew the rabies virus in the brains and spinal cords of rabbits. The rabbits were killed, their spinal cords were removed, dried, and pulverized, and a solution containing the powder was injected into dogs, creating the first vaccine against rabies in dogs (1885). Shortly after Pasteur successfully tested his rabies vaccine, a rabid dog bit a nine-year-old child. Pasteur was able to save the boy from certain death by injecting him thirteen times with the vaccine. (Pasteur also gave the world sterilization, pasteurization, and the germ theory of disease.)

From 1870 to 1925, medical science made great strides in Europe and in the United States. Acceptance of the germ theory of disease led to the discovery of causative organisms for such diseases as yellow fever, diphtheria, and typhoid, and eventually for vaccines for these diseases. (In the late 1800s, the infant mortality rate was reduced from 40 percent to 10 percent in babies infected with diphtheria.) Bacteriology and immunology became recognized sciences, and work progressed along many fronts in the fight against human suffering and disease. Animal testing played a large role in scientific research during this time, as scientists realized that they could often use animals as surrogates for human beings in creating disease models and developing treatments.

In the late nineteenth century and early-to-mid-twentieth century in the United States, animal testing led to:

- **Development of a diphtheria antitoxin (1890); diphtheria vaccine (1923);**

- **The first vaccine for cholera (1879);**

- **A vaccine for plague (1897);**

- **The extraction of hormones for the first time (1902);**

- **Reduction in fatalities from cerebrospinal meningitis (1906);**

- **The development of a chemical treatment for syphilis (1909);**

- **Typhoid fever vaccine (1909);**

- **The isolation of insulin to treat diabetes (1920);**

- **Tuberculosis vaccine (1921);**

- **A vaccine against yellow fever (1935);**

- **A vaccine for typhus (1937);**

- **The creation of a polio vaccine (1952).**

Animals were used in different ways as these discoveries were made. Sometimes disease organisms were injected into the animals to see if symptoms developed or if the organism multiplied inside the bodies of the animals. If the organism multiplied inside the animals' bodies, it was grown in tissue cultures and weakened. After a weakened form of the organism was grown, it was again injected into animals to see if the animals then became resistant to the disease. Sometimes humans volunteered for early trials and then animals were used to produce vaccines, as in early research into the cause of yellow fever and how it was spread.

Not only were animals used in experiments to discover the cause, method of transfer, path, and vaccine for a disease, they were also used in experiments on nutrition:

• **Chickens were used to identify the essential nutrient thiamine. In 1890, Christiaan Eijkman, a prison medical officer in Java, the Dutch East Indies, noticed that chickens fed a diet of polished rice developed a paralytic disease. He and other researchers also discovered that feeding the chickens rice bran cured the disease. The disease was beriberi—caused in both animals and people by a lack of thiamine. Thiamine is found in the rice's bran covering; when the bran is stripped away, the thiamine is lost.**

• **Guinea pigs helped scientists discover vitamin C. As early as 1795, James Lind, a Scottish physician, studied sailors who showed symptoms of scurvy—a bone-weakening disease that killed more than one million sailors between 1600 and 1800. Lind found that sailors ill with scurvy who were given lime juice recovered in a matter of days and could return to work. Those sailors who did not receive lime juice worsened. Scurvy began to disappear among seamen when their diets included limes, lemons, or oranges.**

Later, in 1890, Axel Holst at the University of Christiana in Oslo, Norway, studied scurvy by inducing the disease in guinea pigs. Holst chose guinea pigs to study without knowing that they do not synthesize their own vitamin C. The choice of study animals was fortunate, because humans also do not synthesize their own vitamin C; therefore, Holst's study results were especially applicable to humans. Additional animal studies at the Lister Institute in London during World War I led to the isolation of vitamin C in 1928 and its synthesis in 1932. Other scientists working with animals between 1913 and 1936 discovered vitamins B, D, E, and K.

Animals were used in the past and are used in the present as scientific models for contagious diseases in humans and for such diseases as diabetes, cancer, heart disease, HIV/AIDS, cystic fibrosis, multiple sclerosis, and many other conditions. It is considered unethical and immoral for scientists to experiment on human beings, and, since the end of World War II and the Nuremberg Convention, it has also become illegal in the United States to experiment on humans, except in the case of voluntary clinical trials. For these reasons, scientists use animals to study disease and unhealthy conditions. Animals are of value because:

- **It is often possible to duplicate unhealthy human conditions in one or more species of animal.**

- **Data obtained through well-planned and responsible animal experimentation can be applicable to humans.**

- **Animal experimentation is legal in the United States, as long as researchers follow the provisions of the Animal Welfare Act. Responsible scientists strive to treat animals humanely, and researchers who treat animals inhumanely may lose federal funding for their research and may be charged with animal cruelty under federal and state laws.**

The following chapters explore questions on all sides of the animal testing argument. Should animals be used as

Animal Researchers Awarded The Nobel Prize

Awarded since 1901, the Nobel Prize is the top scientific award in the world. According to the Nobel Foundation, the group that awards the prize, the prizes are given to those who confer the greatest benefit to humanity. The following chart shows a few of the Nobel scientists from the twentieth and twenty-first centuries who have been recognized for their work with animals.

Year	Scientist(s)	Animal(s) Used	Contributions Made
1901	von Behring	Guinea pig	Development of diphtheria antiserum
1902	Ross	Pigeon	Understanding of malaria life cycle
1905	Koch	Cow, sheep	Studies of pathogenesis of tuberculosis
1912	Carrel	Dog	Surgical advances in the suturing and grafting of blood vessels
1923	Banting, Macleod	Dog, rabbit, fish	Discovery of insulin and mechanism of diabetes
1924	Einthoven	Dog	Mechanism of the electrocardiograph
1928	Nicolle	Monkey, pig, rat, mouse	Pathogenesis of typhus
1932	Sherrington, Adrian	Dog, cat	Functions of neurons
1934	Whipple, Murphy, Minot	Dog	Liver therapy for anemia
1945	Fleming, Chain, Florey	Mouse	Curative effect of penicillin in bacterial infections
1947	Carl Cori, Gerty Cori Houssay	Frog, toad, dog	Catalytic conversions of glycogen in the pituitary in sugar metabolism
1951	Theiler	Monkey, mouse	Development of yellow fever vaccine
1954	Enders, Weller, Robbins	Monkey, mouse	Culture of poliovirus that led to development of vaccine
1966	Rous, Huggins	Rat, rabbit, hen	Tumor-inducing viruses and hormonal treatment of cancer
1971	Sutherland	Mammalian liver	Mechanism of the actions of hormones
1986	Levi-Montalcini, Cohen	Mouse, chick, snake	Nerve growth factor and epidermal growth factor
1990	Murray, Thomas	Dog	Organ transplantation techniques
1997	Prusiner	Hamster, mouse	Discovery and characterization of prions
2002	Brenner, Horvitz, Sulston	Roundworm	Genetic regulation of organ development and programmed death

test subjects to the possible benefit of humans and other animals? Do animals have the moral right to live out their lives as nature intended, without human exploitation? Should animals have legal rights to protect them against serving as test subjects? Are present laws regarding the use of animals in testing programs sufficient to protect the animals? Who enforces existing laws? Can test results obtained using nonhuman animals be reliably transferred to humans? Are militant animal protection groups threatening lives by disrupting biomedical studies that use animals? Do most animal experiments constitute valid science, or are they simply sources of cash for research laboratories and scientists?

You don't have to be a scientist to feel strongly about animal testing. No matter what your personal interests are or which profession you pursue, you will no doubt take a stand on this emotionally charged issue, and you may change your position as you gather more information. Deciding where one stands on the issue of animal testing is not always an either-or proposition. Moderates, or people in the middle of the pro-con spectrum, may believe that animal testing is necessary in some instances, as in finding new cures or vaccines for human and animal disease, but not in others—to test cosmetics, for example. The key to helping you form your own opinions about the animal testing controversy is to become informed about all sides of the issue. The information presented here can help you get started.

For and Against

Because animal testing evokes strong emotions, positions held on the issue vary greatly. Most people who object to animal testing cite ethical and moral grounds. They may consider the practice cruel, unjust, misleading, unnecessary, or even dangerous to humans. (Dangerous to humans, for example, because cross-species treatments, such as using pig valves in human hearts, could cause deadly autoimmune reactions.) Members of some groups that are opposed to animal testing and experimentation may also object to hunting and fishing; eating meat or other animal products; wearing fur, feathers, or leather; keeping animals as pets; or using animals for entertainment, as in circuses, zoos, movies, and rodeos. In fact, some people who object to animal testing claim that because animals are living creatures and are sentient (aware) they should have rights, just as humans have rights. Animals should not be exploited for any purpose, they say, including biomedical studies.

Many people who are against animal testing also argue that:

- **It is wasteful—both of dollars and of animals' lives;**

- **Scientists who use animals as test models are doing it for the money they can get in grants;**

- **Nonhuman animals are so different from humans that tests on animals do not reflect how humans would react under the same circumstances;**

- **Handling and caging animals for testing causes so much stress in the animal that test results are unreliable;**

- **There are experimental methods available to scientists that do not require the use of animals.**

According to C. Ray Greek, M.D., president and founder of Americans For Medical Advancement (AFMA), a large percentage of scientists who are not engaged in research using animals believe that animal testing and experimentation have little or no value in today's world. "We don't have ethical issues with animal research," Greek says of the membership of AFMA. "Our issues are human-related, in that we don't think experiments on animals are going to result in cures for cancer, AIDS, multiple sclerosis, or other diseases. We approach the issue strictly from a scientific perspective, saying that experiments on animals have outlived their usefulness and do more harm than good."

As the authors of three books for the general public, Greek and his wife, Jean Swingle Greek, D.V.M., researched the history of animal experimentation and concluded that many accounts—such as animal research leading to microbiologist Sir Alexander Fleming's discovery of penicillin and Louis Pasteur's development of the first rabies vaccine, are not completely accurate, in that animal testing did not benefit either project. The AFMA Web site publishes detailed accounts of the Greeks' views of these historic events and others, but Ray Greek points out that the emphasis should not be on the past, but on the present and future. "In the 1880s we studied dogs and other animals, and that helped us figure out what the pancreas did," Greek illustrates. "In the 1880s, that's where medical science was. My wife and I have written two books about how the animal model is just flat out wrong—it gets it wrong more often than it gets it right. Therefore, the model, as a paradigm [example] should be abandoned. It's like the gun that doesn't shoot straight."

What can researchers do instead of animal experimentation? The Greeks answer that question in their most recent book for the general public, *What Will We Do if We Don't Experiment on Animals?* Alternatives are suggested, and many are listed in Chapter 9, "Alternatives to Animal Testing." We can use computer models, in vitro procedures, and other alternatives, Ray Greek says, but

> **none of these things will accurately predict human responses 100 percent of the time. Right now, for example, the animal models that address toxicity testing get it right around 5 to 25 percent of the time. Computer models get it right more like 70 to 90 percent of the time. So it's true that we don't have anything in science today that will tell me with 100 percent accuracy what a drug is going to do when I use it. But it's fallacious [misleading] to say that for this reason we should experiment on animals, because, again, the animal models get it right less frequently than the computer models.**

At the molecular level, where genetic differences between individuals and species reside, Greek sums up, studies focusing on animal models are of little value, and testing toxicity reactions in animals is not a reliable predictor of how the same toxic substances will affect people.

Today we know that identical twins do not necessarily react the same way to the same medication. So if identical twins cannot predict for each other, how in the world are we going to predict based on testing in a rat, monkey, or [other nonhuman animal]? Greek asks.

Scientists and others on the pro side of the argument counter that historical records of beneficial animal testing are largely accurate, and that there are many scientific and medical advantages afforded humans and nonhuman animals from animal testing that should outweigh objections. Without animal testing, they point out, many lifesaving vaccines, drugs, and surgical procedures would never have been developed. And with the potential for genetic engineering exploding, manipulating animal and human genomes may provide a way to eliminate many hereditary diseases that have plagued people for centuries—diseases such as cystic fibrosis, hemophilia, sickle cell anemia, and certain forms of cancer. (A genome consists of all the genes found in an animal's cells.)

Furthermore, most research scientists are aware that stress can skew test results, and, consequently, they handle animal subjects humanely. In addition, layers of federal and state laws now mandate the humane treatment of laboratory animals, and there are penalties for those who disobey the law—not the least of which is withdrawal of funding for research.

The "cash cow" argument doesn't make sense, says Greg Popken, a postdoctoral research fellow in pediatric endocrinology at the University of North Carolina in Chapel Hill. "I'm not making much money. I have friends with bachelor's degrees who earn much more than I do with a Ph.D. [Biomedical research] is a small percentage of the health care dollar. About three cents of every dollar spent for health care is actually spent on research of all types—clinical, animal, in vitro, and so on."

"Animal research is an extended business, both because of regulations and because it's important to carefully control the environments the animals are maintained in, so you don't get unexpected results to variables that aren't part of the study," adds B. Taylor Bennett, a laboratory veterinarian and director of the University of Illinois' Biologic Resources Laboratory. "I don't know of any university or company that gets much of a return on their investment for what it costs to do animal research. . . . Nobody is getting rich off of [animal research]."

Money does drive animal research projects, argues Ray Greek. Scientists cling to animal models in their research "because that's the only thing they know how to do. Most of [the argument] is not about science. If you talk to people in the scientific community who don't have a vested interest in animal experimentation, you'll find there is almost 100 percent agreement that the paradigm itself has outlived its usefulness. The people who scream the loudest that we have to do [animal experimentation] are the people whose mortgages are being paid because of experiments on animals."

Alternative testing methods, such as computer models and tissue cultures, may supplement existing live animal techniques, but they cannot completely replace animal studies, argue proponents of animal testing. (Alternatives are discussed in more detail in Chapter 9.)

Those who argue in favor of animal testing also point out that animal experimentation is not always based on animals' similarity to humans. Sometimes it is the differences that matter. For example, animal testing is performed to learn such secrets as why sharks are resistant to cancer, how amphibians regulate their own blood pressure, and the mechanism used by cockroaches to regenerate severed nerves that run from the insect's body to its leg. Knowledge obtained through working with these animals and others could relieve or prevent much human disease and suffering, argue proponents of testing.

Those in favor of animal testing also claim that the medical procedures, drugs, and other advances often benefit animals as well as humans. For example, the surgical technique for repairing holes in the hearts of children is also used successfully on puppies suffering from the same congenital (inherited) heart deformity. Dogs can be fitted with heart pacemakers. And hip problems in large dogs can often be repaired using the same hip surgery techniques used in people. Furthermore, plastic surgery techniques used on people may also restore an injured and scarred thoroughbred horse to its former beauty.

In addition, vaccines for animal diseases exist because of animal testing. For instance, animals can now be treated for hookworm, heartworm, Giardia, tuberculosis, rickets, white muscle disease, brain tumors, birth defects, and cancer. Animal research has saved dogs from distemper, Parvovirus, infectious hepatitis, parainfluenza, and leptospirosis. It has saved cats from rhinotracheitis, pneumonitis, feline leukemia, enteritis, and dilated cardiomyopathy. Animal research has also resulted in treatments for poultry with Newcastle disease, Marek's disease, fowl cholera, duck hepatitis, hemorrhagic enteritis, fowl typhoid, and fowl pox. The list of veterinary benefits continues: horses with strangles, tetanus, and encephalomyelitis; sheep with anthrax and bluetongue; and pigs with influenza and swine erysipelas.

Despite beneficial developments in human and animal medicine that many attribute to animal testing and experimentation, the debate continues to be largely emotional because many people keep animals as pets and develop close attachments to them. People also admire the beauty and independence of wild animals. Most animal welfare advocates, including a majority of biomedical researchers, would agree that these are valid reasons for treating animals humanely and for helping to preserve their natural environments. They also agree that since humans are moral beings, they have a moral obligation to treat animals humanely. According to some scientists, these principles are not at odds with animal experimentation.

The fundamental principle of the animal rights movement is that nonhuman animals deserve to live according to their own needs, free from abuse, unnecessary pain and suffering, and exploitation. For most groups whose members champion animal rights, this means:

- **Keeping domestic animals, such as cats and dogs, as companion animals, but never cutting off tails and ears, and never attempting to keep wild animals or birds in homes;**

- **Providing for the physical and psychological needs of all domestic animals;**

- **Spaying and neutering pets to avoid adding to the world's population of unwanted animals;**

- **Eliminating the practice of breeding animals to be sold as pets;**

- **Never exploiting animals for entertainment, such as in circuses, zoos, and rodeos;**

- **Never fishing or hunting animals;**

- **Not wearing fur, feathers, leather, or any other animal-derived material;**

- **Not eating meat, fish, or animal products;**

- **Never testing or experimenting on animals.**

Some animal rights groups may advocate civil disobedience to draw attention to the cause, while others do not. And some animal rights groups advocate and practice violence—such as throwing paint on fur garments; vandalizing research labs; using bombs and committing arson; and harassing employees of targeted animal labs, pet food manufacturers, and related enterprises—as the only way to get others to listen.

Two animal rights groups that are often in the news are The Animal Liberation Front (ALF) and People for the Ethical Treatment of Animals (PETA). The ALF began in Great Britain in 1976, the year after Peter Singer's book was published. The ALF was founded by Ronnie Lee, who had reportedly served time in prison in 1974 and again in 1977 after being caught during laboratory break-ins that were somehow connected with protecting animals from abuse. The ALF spread to Germany, the Netherlands, France, Spain, Italy, Australia, Canada, Poland, and South Africa; its American branch was formed in 1982.

The ALF has no headquarters and no official membership list, but other groups allegedly support The ALF's activities, including the Animal Liberation Front Support Group of America, Last Chance for Animals, and PETA, the latter to the extent of providing legal representation for some individuals who have been arrested. The ALF groups have apparently taken credit, both in Great Britain and in the United States, for acts such as laboratory break-ins, theft and destruction of laboratory property and scientists' records, theft of research animals, arson, and harassment of scientists and corporate employees who work for companies associated with animal research. As a result, it is on the Federal Bureau of Investigation's list of domestic terrorists. (When the initials "ALF" are spray-painted or otherwise left at the scene, the group is assumed to have been responsible, and sometimes group members themselves tell the news media of their actions.)

The ALF's stated aims are:

- **To free animals from places of abuse, such as scientific laboratories, factory farms, fur farms, and so on, and place them in homes where they can live out their lives free from suffering;**

- **To inflict economic damage on those who exploit animals and/or cause them to suffer;**

- **To reveal harmful acts committed against animals behind locked doors, by performing nonviolent liberations (freeing research animals) and other direct actions;**

- **To take all necessary precautions against harming any animal, human and nonhuman.**

Alex Pacheco, a college student, and Ingrid Newkirk, a former policewoman, co-founded People for the Ethical Treatment of Animals (PETA) in 1980; by 2004, the animal rights organization had 800,000 members. PETA's Web site states:

PETA operates under the simple principle that animals are not ours to eat, wear, experiment on, or use for entertainment.

PETA focuses its attention on the four areas in which the largest numbers of animals suffer the most intensely for the longest periods of time: on factory farms, in laboratories, in the fur trade, and in the entertainment industry. We also work on a variety of other issues, including the cruel killing of beavers, birds and other 'pests,' and the abuse of backyard dogs.

Some PETA members campaign to:

• **Eliminate the meat industry;**

• **Prohibit the use of furs from fur farms or wild animals;**

• **Stop all hunting;**

• **Stop all fishing;**

• **Stop the use of animals in entertainment, medical research, and military research;**

• **Prevent the use of all animal products such as wool;**

• **Stop the breeding of animals for pets.**

PETA claims not to support violent tactics in their efforts on behalf of animals, but the group does not condemn the ALF's alleged criminal activity. In response to the question, "How can you justify the millions of dollars in property damage caused by the ALF?" the PETA Web page published this response in September 2004:

Throughout history, some people have felt the need to break the law to fight injustice. The Underground Railroad and the French Resistance are examples of movements in which people broke the law in order to answer to a higher morality. The ALF, which is simply the name adopted by people who act illegally in behalf of animal rights, breaks inanimate objects such as stereotaxic devices and decapitators in order to save lives. ALF members burn empty buildings in which animals are tortured and killed. ALF "raids" have given us proof of horrific cruelty that would not have otherwise been discovered or believed and have resulted in criminal charges' being filed against laboratories for violations of the Animal Welfare Act. Often, ALF raids have been followed by widespread scientific con-

demnation of the practices occurring in the targeted labs, and some abusive laboratories have been permanently shut down as a result.

Distinguishing between animal welfare groups and groups devoted to animal rights can help clarify the issue, but differences are not absolute. That is, members of any group concerned with animals may follow individual goals and practices not typical of the group as a whole. For example, a member of PETA or the Humane Society of the United States doesn't necessarily participate in sit-ins or carry protest signs in a demonstration, yet both groups condone nonviolent protests against animal cruelty.

Here is how two groups concerned with eliminating animal cruelty express the difference.

PETA calls itself an animal *rights* organization, as opposed to an animal *welfare* organization, and distinguishes between the two as follows: "Animal welfare theories accept that animals have interests, but allow these interests to be traded away as long as there are some human benefits that are thought to justify that sacrifice." In other words, says Lisa Lange, vice president of communications for PETA, "animal rights groups, like PETA, Compassion Over Killing, and Farm Sanctuary have as their goal the abolition of all animal abuse—whether the abuse is caging animals, experimenting on them and killing them, raising them for fur and breaking their necks, factory farms, or slaughterhouses. Animal welfare organizations may simply want to improve animal welfare on farms, in slaughterhouses, and in the laboratory. A simple way of putting it is that animal welfare is advocating for larger cages. Animal rights activists are asking for empty cages."

The National Animal Interest Alliance, an animal welfare group, makes this distinction:

Animal welfare requires humane treatment of animals on farms and ranches, in circuses and

rodeos, and in homes, kennels, catteries, laboratories, and wherever else animals are kept. Animal welfare endorses quick death when death is inevitable and a scientific approach to commercial use and management of wild populations. . . .

Animal rights works for the day when we will have no interactions with animals but will view them from afar.

While PETA, the ALF, and other animal rights groups hope to eventually halt all biomedical research using animals, many scientists and more moderate animal welfare groups hope that morals, ethical principles and guidelines, and laws with penalties for violation will eliminate those researchers practicing bad science without putting an end to vital research. Scientists who work with animals see first-hand the benefits of such work, but they realize that, just as in any profession, those members of the scientific community who are careless with the animals in their charge, or who put science before the humane treatment of animals, can damage the reputations of all scientists engaged in animal research.

One such situation involved the Coulston Foundation (TCF), a private contract testing facility established by toxicologist Fred Coulston in Alamogordo, New Mexico, in 1980. In 1988, the laboratory advertised the availability of its chimpanzees and monkeys for developing cosmetics and insecticides, and for biomedical experiments. By 1993, the Coulston Foundation controlled more than 500 chimpanzees, making it the world's largest captive chimpanzee colony. The animals at the site included 141 Air Force chimpanzees that had been used in space flight research.

After several incidents of chimpanzees and monkeys dying from overheating, lack of water, and inadequate veterinary care, the U.S. Department of Agriculture (USDA)

THE UNITED STATES DEPARTMENT OF AGRICULTURE FILED CHARGES OF ANIMAL ABUSE AGAINST THE COULSTON FOUNDATION IN NEW MEXICO, AND THE FACILITY EVENTUALLY DECLARED BANKRUPTCY AND CLOSED IN 2002.

filed formal charges against TCF. After the USDA had filed formal charges of animal abuse against the lab three times, it was finally forced into bankruptcy and closed in 2002. Many of the 327 animals housed there at the time the facility closed found permanent homes in refuge facilities for "retired" laboratory primates, including Primarily Primates in Texas, and the Fort Pierce, Florida-based Center for Captive Chimpanzee Care (CCCC), founded by Jane Goodall, Roger Fouts, and Carole Noon. The Center for Captive Chimpanzee Care received a $3.7 million grant from the Arcus Foundation in Kalamazoo, Michigan, enabling CCCC to buy the Coulston property, on condition that TCF donate all the primates left in the facility to the Florida sanctuary. Several animal protection organizations contributed financial support toward the closure of TCF, including the Animal Rights Foundation of Florida, Doris Day Animal League, Friends of Washoe, New England Anti-Vivisection Society, and In Defense of Animals.

In Defense of Animals (IDA), an animal rights organization based in Mill Valley, California, began a campaign against the Coulston Foundation in 1993, after hearing of its many violations of the Animal Welfare Act. In addition to providing financial support for the purchase of the foundation, the organization is credited with petitioning the government to close the facility, keeping the dismal situation before the public, and helping to find refuge for the primates housed there.

Similarly, Roger Fouts, a cofounder of CCCC and a psychology professor at Central Washington University in Ellensburg, became an animal welfare advocate after witnessing what he considered inhumane treatment of chimpanzees and monkeys in certain laboratory facilities in the 1980s.

Through the 1970s, 1980s, and 1990s, Fouts had designed and implemented programs to communicate with chimpanzees in American Sign Language (ASL). (ASL consists of hand signals used in hearing-impaired communication.)

Koko and Washoe Learn ASL

JANE GOODALL IS FAMOUS FOR HER STUDY OF CHIMPANZEES IN THE WILD AND FOR HER COMPASSION FOR PRIMATES. HERE, SHE COMMUNICATES WITH A BABY CHIMPANZEE IN JULY 1994 AT THE GOMBE STREAM NATIONAL PARK IN TANZANIA.

Koko the gorilla was just a baby when Penny Patterson, Ph.D., president and director of research for the Gorilla Foundation, began teaching her American Sign Language. Now thirty-three, Koko knows over 1,000 signs, and recently "told" her caregivers at the Woodside, California, Ape Preserve that she had a toothache. Koko received dental treatment and a complete physical. She was found to be in good health and able to have a baby, which keepers say is her "greatest desire."

Visit this Web site to see forty-eight of Koko's favorite signs: http://www.koko.org/world/signlanguage.html.

Dr. Fouts' friend, Washoe, born in 1965, was the first chimpanzee to learn American Sign Language. Find out more about Fouts's chimpanzees at http://www.friendsofwashoe.org/chcichimps/meet-thechimps.htm.

While his experiments involved discovering how adept chimpanzees could become at communicating with humans using ASL, the animals' welfare was always his primary goal. Whenever possible over the years, Fouts has chosen career directions that do not sacrifice his animals or their relationships—both human and primate. He treats his chimpanzee subjects with affection and respect and considers them family members.

In his 1997 book, *Next of Kin,* Fouts tells of a 1987 visit to a Maryland biomedical laboratory that used chimpanzees as test subjects. Fouts was disturbed at the lack of compassion displayed by the scientists and animal keepers. The chimps were kept in tiny metal and Plexiglas isolettes with respirators on top. They could barely turn around, and each cage contained just one animal. This prevented the chimps, normally social animals, from interacting with other chimpanzees. "I'll never forget the moment we saw our first chimpanzee in one of [the cages]," Fouts recalls. "The young chimpanzee was clinging in despair to the bottom of this small container. When we opened the door she turned her head toward us. But when she looked at us she seemed to look right through us. She was mentally gone." Jane Goodall, the famous chimpanzee researcher, accompanied Fouts on this trip. As they left the facility, Fouts asked her how humans could treat chimpanzees this way. Goodall, with tears in her eyes, responded with a line from Shakespeare, "All pity choked by custom of fell deed." Scientific objectivity had replaced compassion in the people working with the chimpanzees.

In 1992, Fouts finally realized his dream of building a chimpanzee-friendly facility to house his famous signing chimps when the spacious Chimpanzee and Human Communication Institute was opened on the CWU campus. In their new complex, Fouts' four remaining chimpanzees communicate with him, his students, and visitors to the center. Fouts' chimpanzees are living out their days in contentment and relative freedom. Fouts and his wife have become devout animal welfare advocates, and they emphasize that animals should never be used simply as "furry test tubes." (When asked about Fouts's work, PETA's Lisa Lange replied, "We love Roger Fouts. He has done so much to further the cause of great apes, and all animals. . . . If we could snap our fingers and have every person who is experimenting on chimpanzees give consideration to the things Roger Fouts had found to be true of these animals, the world would be a kinder and safer place for these animals.")

The contrast between the biomedical laboratory Fouts visited and his own program is stark. Clearly, personal experiences and media reports influence one's perception of animal testing and experimentation, and help mold one's views of the practice. However, according to the research scientists quoted in this text, rarely do biomedical research programs totally disregard the humane treatment of their animal subjects, since current federal laws mandating accountability were written to prevent this. In addition, researchers who do not consider the welfare of their animal charges can invalidate their own test results, and they can lose federal funding for their research projects. Unfortunately, horror stories of animal abuse make sensational headlines, while those programs that are animal-friendly seldom make the news.

While considering the animal testing issue, it's important to remember that there are many sides to the argument, and there are many individuals on all sides who treat animals humanely and with respect, and who sincerely want to help animals without sacrificing the welfare of people.

3

Animals Used in Testing

Statistics vary greatly for the number of animals used in testing and research annually in the United States, but several estimates put the total number at 17 to 22 million; a decrease of 40 percent since 1968. (Numbers vary according to sources collecting statistics: government figures tend to be lower than those published by animal rights and welfare groups.) Rats, mice, and other rodents make up 95 percent of all animals used, and primates (monkeys, gorillas, orangutans, and chimpanzees) make up one-third of one percent of all animals used.

Chimpanzees are humans' closest living nonhuman relatives. Their genetic make-up is approximately 99 percent the same as ours. For this reason, they have been used extensively to study infectious diseases and other medical conditions, as well as the effects of space travel. This genetic similarity led scientists to believe that chimpanzees would react to infectious diseases—especially HIV/AIDS—the same as humans react. Because of the widespread use of chimpanzees to study HIV/AIDS, from the mid-1980s to the mid-1990s, the National Institutes of Health (NIH) funded a captive chimpanzee-breeding program for HIV/AIDS research. Chimpanzees, however, were found to be unsuitable models for HIV research because, although they harbor the virus, they do not develop AIDS symptoms. (Although other species do not develop AIDS from HIV, there are similar diseases they do acquire: simian monkeys can develop Simian Immunodeficiency Virus; cats can become infected with Feline Immunodeficiency Virus; and cattle can suffer from the disease caused by Bovine Immunodeficiency Virus.)

The discovery that chimpanzees did not develop AIDS from HIV led to a surplus of the animals, as demonstrated by the fact that in 2003 an estimated 1,600 to 1,700 chimpanzees were housed in American laboratories.

Because of the growing chimpanzee surplus, in 1997 the National Research Council (NRC) advised the federal government to stop chimpanzee-breeding programs. The government was urged to work with private donors to fund sanctuaries for retired laboratory chimpanzees. In December 2000, President Bill Clinton signed the CHIMP Act, which provides the federal funding needed to establish a chimpanzee sanctuary system in which the animals can be kept in an environment simulating their natural habitat.

Increasingly, animals other than primates are used as test subjects in many studies because primates are not always the best animal models for studies, as in HIV, and because there are shortages of some primates other than chimpanzees. For instance, in August 2003, national newspapers reported a shortage of rhesus macaques for use in biomedical research. Macaques are a species of monkey with about 92 percent genetic similarity to humans, and they are used in such research as genetic mapping, organ transplant techniques, and how stem cells can be used to help humans with certain diseases. The shortage meant

THIS BABY RED-TAILED MACAQUE WAS USED IN **AIDS** RESEARCH AT
THE UNIVERSITY OF WASHINGTON IN SEATTLE IN **1992.**

that the price of one rhesus macaque could be as high as $10,000 when the animals were purchased from research animal breeders.

There are other reasons fewer primates are being used in biomedical research:

- **Primates are more expensive to buy and maintain than other animals.**

- **Primates have long life spans, and they do not reproduce quickly, which means that the animals must be properly maintained for long periods of time, and it takes a long time to process results over several generations.**

- **Because of their similarity to humans, there is widespread objection among animal welfare groups and the general public to using primates as research subjects.**

Nonhuman animals other than primates that are most commonly used in testing include rodents (rats, mice, gerbils, hamsters, and guinea pigs), rabbits, dogs, cats, fish, frogs, birds (chickens and pigeons), sheep, and pigs. Many animals used in testing are supplied for research through breeding programs or commercial animal supply companies.

A policy called pound seizure, enacted by law in several states, allows research laboratories to take animals held by city pounds if owners do not claim them within a certain time period. A pound is a facility established by city ordinance where unwanted or stray animals are "impounded" (kept). If animals are not claimed or adopted within specified time periods, typically ranging from seven days to thirty days, they are painlessly and quickly put to death, because pounds cannot afford to keep such animals indefinitely. (The total annual cost of pet control in the

United States is more than $500 million, and taxpayers bear most of the cost.)

Fewer than 2 percent of the ten million pound animals that are put to death each year are used for medical research. Forty-nine states currently allow some form of pound animal use for research and education—Massachusetts is the only state that does not. Twelve states—Connecticut, Delaware, Hawaii, Maine, Maryland, New Hampshire, New Jersey, New York, Pennsylvania, Rhode Island, Vermont, and West Virginia—permit the use of animals originating from out-of-state pounds, but do not allow pounds within state borders to release unwanted animals to research and teaching institutions.

Despite rumors to the contrary, stray pets found wandering city streets are not routinely captured for use in animal testing and research laboratories. Strays are not desirable test and research subjects because:

- **An estimated 95 percent of all animals used for research and testing are rodents. Cats and dogs together make up less than one-half of one percent of all lab animals.**

- **Animals are most often bred especially for research purposes and were never pets, unless they are obtained from states that allow pounds to sell unclaimed animals for research purposes. The most recent USDA figures indicate that in 2002, 92,475 dogs and cats together were used in medical research. Compare those numbers to these: Over seven million unclaimed dogs and cats are euthanized in animal shelters every year. Wildlife biologists estimate that over one million animals are killed every day by cars.**

- **Strict federal laws prohibit stealing pets for research. According to the Animal Welfare Act, it is a federal offense to "buy, sell, exhibit, use for research, transport or offer for transportation any stolen animal" or to obtain "live random source dogs and cats" through false pretenses, misrepresentation, or deception. Certain breeders, categorized as "Class B" breeders, may be licensed to sell animals to research facilities. They can obtain animals from pounds in those states that allow pound seizure, but only after holding periods are met, both by the pounds and the breeders. Class B breeders are subject to USDA inspection four times a year. They must keep thorough records, including specific descriptions of each animal and details regarding the animal's source. Violations result in fines or license suspension or revocation.**

Mice and rats are replacing larger animals, such as dogs and cats, for testing, because they breed quickly, have shorter life spans, are relatively easy to handle and keep, and can be manipulated at the molecular level. In addition, studies comparing the genetic makeup of humans to that of mice have found that the human and mouse genomes are similar.

Specially bred mice are used extensively in animal testing programs. Called knockout and transgenic mice, the rodents are genetically engineered. To create knockout mice, scientists "knock out" or remove certain genes to prevent their effects from being expressed. Scientists create transgenic mice by adding foreign genetic material to the rodent's DNA sequence. (DNA—deoxyribonucleic acid—is the protein within an organism's cells that makes up its

Most animal rights and animal welfare advocates hope to see the day when animals like these white rats are no longer caged for testing or experimentation.

genes and chromosomes and determines which traits will be expressed.)

To create transgenic mice, eggs are taken from female mice and injected with transgenes, which are bits of foreign genetic material. The fertilized, genetically engineered eggs are then implanted in the uteruses of female mice. Some develop to term and are born with the injected DNA firmly in place. Transgenic mice might carry DNA from any one of a variety of organisms, from viruses to humans. Laboratories may raise their own mice, or commercial animal laboratories supply these mice to testing programs, guaranteeing their genetic purity, and usually guaranteeing that they are pathogen free.

Transgenic mice are often bred for use in specific studies. For example, mice genetically engineered to carry the human gene APOA1 produce a protein component of the good HDL cholesterol. (People produce two kinds of cholesterol—a fatty protein, LDL cholesterol is most likely to clog arteries and lead to heart disease and stroke. HDL cholesterol, on the other hand, can actually help prevent heart attacks when present in high levels by helping to remove LDL cholesterol from the body.) These mice are unusually resistant to heart disease, so they are used in studies to learn how HDL cholesterol protects people from heart attacks.

Transgenic rats have also been created—a more difficult process than creating transgenic mice—and are used in studies of such diseases as diabetes and cancer.

How closely related are humans to mice? Mice, humans, and all mammals, including dogs, cats, rats, rabbits, and primates, contain almost the same number of genes, now estimated at 25,000. Similarities between mouse and human genes range from about 70 percent to 98.2 percent, with an average of 85 percent similarity. Some mouse and human genes produce identical actions in both species, while others are exclusively mouse or human, such as length of tail in a mouse or height in people.

Since federal law requires that drugs be tested in humans before they are released for sale, paid and unpaid human volunteers are used for many biomedical studies and clinical trials. Laws governing medical care in the United States say that people must be well informed about biomedical studies and clinical trials before they agree to participate, and must sign forms indicating that they understand the process, have been duly informed, and agree to participate.

Industries and organizations that routinely conduct

animal testing include the chemical and biomedical industries, and educational institutions. Chemical and environmental scientists conduct toxicity tests for chemicals used in agricultural, industrial, and household products.

The National Toxicology Program (NTP), in existence since 1978, uses rodents and some in vitro studies to predict human cancer risks from certain chemicals and their by-products. (*In vitro* studies involve studying live cells in a test tube, instead of using a live animal.)

Scientists for the biomedical industry test new drugs, surgical techniques, medical equipment, and other devices and products used in medical science. Biomedical researchers also conduct experiments designed to study a human disease or condition that can be duplicated or simulated in certain animal species.

Educational institutions conduct noninvasive animal research, such as Fouts's chimpanzee communication studies, and also sponsor more invasive studies in physiology, anatomy, and other branches of science. At all levels, teachers may guide students in performing experiments, including dissection and/or surgery on living and dead animals as part of various educational curricula.

When animals are used in place of humans in test situations, scientists try to determine whether or not the test data will be duplicated in humans. Will substances that cause cancer in mice also cause the disease in humans? If so, does a specific amount of a substance that causes cancer in a mouse that weighs a few ounces also cause cancer in a person who weighs 150 pounds? How do scientists transfer data obtained through animal testing to people? Complicated mathematical formulas—sometimes several pages long—are used to calculate the likelihood of test results in animals being duplicated in humans. The accuracy of this process is also questioned by animal welfare and animal rights groups.

The Tuskegee Experiment

For forty years between 1932 and 1972, the United States government conducted an experiment on 399 African-American men with syphilis, a sexually transmitted disease that can be fatal if untreated. The men were poor and some were illiterate. They were never told that they had syphilis. Instead, the doctors observing them told them they suffered from "bad blood," and did nothing to stop the ravages of the disease, which include painful sores, tumors, blindness, paralysis, insanity, and death.

The purpose of the experiment was supposedly to study how syphilis affects African Americans, as opposed to the white population, but benefits were finally shown to be nonexistent. Because the men were observed but not aggressively treated, they were prevented from getting effective medical care, with the result that twenty-eight died directly of syphilis, one hundred died of related complications, forty wives were infected, and nineteen children were born with congenital syphilis.

Jean Heller of the Associated Press exposed the Tuskegee, Alabama, experiment in a July 25, 1972, article in the *Washington Star*. Under the glare of exposure the government stopped the experiment, and for the first time the men who participated received effective medical treatment for syphilis. A lawsuit resulted in a $10 million settlement for the men and their families.

On May 16, 1997, U.S. President Bill Clinton apologized to the eight remaining survivors of the Tuskegee Experiment:

> **The United States government did something that was wrong—deeply, profoundly, morally wrong. It was an outrage to our commitment to integrity and equality for all our citizens . . . clearly racist.**

Aside from the ethical and moral issue of the humane treatment of animals used in testing is the issue of valid science. Are animal tests a valid way to learn how human body systems will respond? A large percentage of research scientists say yes, but Ray and Jean Greek of Americans for Medical Advancement, say no. In *Specious Science: How Genetics and Evolution Reveal Why Medical Research on Animals Harms Humans*, they state:

> **If every nonhuman animal species never or rarely reacted the same way as humans, or, conversely, if they always or almost always reacted the same way as humans, they might be useful. But since animals react in the same way as humans in an unreliable, unpredictable manner, animals are dangerous models for humans. Moreover, it is impossible to know which animal will respond in the same way a human does until it is known how a human responds. It is knowledge after the fact—redundant, and therefore useless.**

The Greeks point to two historical examples to support their argument. "In animal tests involving thalidomide and penicillin, some animal species were found to react to these drugs in the same way as humans," they say. White New Zealand rabbits, for example, gave birth to deformed offspring when given twenty-five to three hundred times the dosage of thalidomide that was given to humans. Other animal species, including mice, did not give birth to deformed offspring after being given thalidomide. (Thalidomide was given to pregnant women to help them sleep. Tragically, it caused some 10,000 human babies to be born with flipper-like arms and legs, or no arms and legs.)

Opponents of animal testing often use the thalidomide argument to illustrate its fallacies. However, the drug was never marketed in the United States, and testing was begun in the United States only after problems appeared in other countries where the drug was marketed. Tests on pregnant animals were not performed before thalidomide was placed on the market in Europe.

In 1929, the Greeks continue, "Alexander Fleming tested penicillin on rabbits; because it did not work on a systemic infection in a rabbit, he set the chemical aside, believing it to be ineffective. Mice were just the opposite. Mice reacted to penicillin as humans did." Consequently, the Greeks maintain, if Fleming had used only the rabbit test as an indication of the efficacy of penicillin, the drug might never have reached the public.

However, counters Robert Speth, a professor of pharmacology and neuroscience at the College of Veterinary Medicine at Washington State University in Pullman and a past president of the Society for Veterinary Medical Ethics, it was Sir Howard Florey in 1940 who used eight mice to demonstrate that penicillin cured streptococcal infections. With Fleming and Chain, he won the Nobel Prize for his efforts, and penicillin was credited with saving the lives of countless soldiers during World War II.

Also counter to the Greeks' argument, states Greg Popken of the University of North Carolina at Chapel Hill, is that Fleming didn't give his "mold juice" (penicillin) to an infected rabbit.

He gave it to a healthy rabbit to test toxicity. Relying on his in vitro (culture dish) data and the excretion rate in the rabbit, he concluded that [his mold juice] would not work systemically. The standard test at the time was to infect animals (usually mice) with bacteria and then administer the drug. Fleming never did this in mice or any other animal. Both he and his boss were skeptical of animal research data. It wasn't until Florey's group in Oxford did it ten years later that the value of penicillin was realized.

According to the Greeks, who advocate the replacement of animals with other testing and experimental procedures, there are also serious risks to humans involved in using animal tissues—in culture mediums, as heart valves, for insulin, to produce antibodies, and so on. Not only do animal tissues fail to react like human tissues, they claim, in many cases, human bodies persistently reject animal tissue when it has been tried for transplants. Moreover, animal tissue can carry disease organisms that infect humans, such as the prions (protein particles) recently discovered as the infectious agents in Mad Cow disease.

The most promising xenotransplantation (the use of animal tissue in humans) research to date involves inserting the genes for certain human proteins and antigens into certain animal genomes (eggs and sperm), such as the pig genome, and then cloning the tissue. Cloning is the process of making exact replicas on one parent cell, and is a faster and less expensive method of producing transgenic animals. Cloning can also limit the possibility of animal viruses or other pathogens being passed on to humans during transplantation. This process would also eliminate instantaneous rejection of the animal tissue that now occurs when animal organs or tissue are transplanted into humans.

Some scientists see the possibility that xenotransplantation could eventually relieve the human organ shortage. As of July 2004, in the United States alone, according to the United Network for Organ Sharing, 86,063 people were on a waiting list for organ transplants. (Waiting list figures are updated hourly.) Since there are not nearly enough organ donors to provide the needed organs, half of those on the transplant waiting list die before a donor is found. Animal rights advocates and some animal welfare groups are against using animals for this purpose, claiming that a mandatory human organ donor system would be a more suitable alternative.

THESE CLONED PIGS WERE TO BE USED FOR TRANSPLANT RESEARCH AT THE VIRGINIA TECH UNIVERSITY RESEARCH FACILITY IN BLACKBURG.

Animal studies can yield results that are reliable indicators of human reactions, if the right animals are tested, says John D. Young, V.M.S., M.S., a laboratory veterinarian, director of the Department of Comparative Medicine at the Cedars-Sinai Medical Center in Los Angeles, and chairman of Americans for Medical Progress. A large part of Young's job, he says, is helping physicians and other scientists choose the appropriate animal species for a study, so that data are more likely to be accurate for humans. If a physician wants to study gall bladders, for example, Young would counsel him or her not to use rats or horses as study subjects: "Rats and horses don't have gall bladders." In addition, Young illustrates, "Pigs and dogs have cardiophysiology/circulatory systems similar to that of humans. So if a physician wants to study cardiopathology [heart disease], he could use pigs or dogs."

Young's job also involves serving as director of the Institutional Animal Care and Use Committee at his research facility and ensuring that federal regulations are followed in the research laboratory he directs.

Do we really need animals for testing? A majority of scientists say that we do. They argue that because scientists have worked on ways to reduce the numbers of animals needed for product safety testing and for biomedical research, many fewer animals are now needed. (Since 1973, the first reporting year after enactment of the Animal Welfare Act, the number of animals used in research of all types has dropped by a little more than 25 percent. Since 1968, the estimated drop in the number of animals is about 40 percent.)

These figures have led some people to believe that for every animal test once performed, there is now an alternative method. This is not true, research scientists claim. In fact, the U.S. Food and Drug Administration (FDA) has issued the following statement concerning alternative tests:

> **[M]any procedures intended to replace animal tests are still in various stages of development and . . . it would be unwise for us to urge manufacturers not to do any further [animal] testing. . . . While the best means may begin with valuable adjunct tests, ultimately testing must progress to a whole intact, living system—an animal.**

While it's true that consumers feel more secure when they know that the government requires new drugs, vaccines, medical techniques, and chemicals used in products to be tested for safety before their use on humans, it's also true that the desire for security is often offset by the public's increasing concern for animal welfare.

Product Safety Testing

Americans are exposed to hundreds of thousands of chemicals daily. Some occur naturally in the environment or are released as industrial by-products. Others are added to food to prevent spoilage or enhance taste. Many are found as ingredients in personal and household products, such as cosmetics, air and hair sprays, bath products, soaps and detergents, and cleaning supplies. Even our clothing is full of chemicals, such as dyes, softeners, and anti-shrink agents. Agricultural chemicals include fertilizers, growth hormones, insecticides, fungicides, herbicides, and rodent poisons. Other chemicals are used as prescription or over-the-counter drugs.

Primarily through animal testing, we know that some of these chemicals are harmful to health. Standardized animal tests are performed to test the toxicity of these chemicals both in the environment and before they are used in products offered for sale to the public.

The purpose of product safety testing is not only to discover which products are safe when used as directed, but also

THESE ANIMAL WELFARE ADVOCATES ARE VOTING AGAINST ANIMAL TESTING OF L'ORÉAL COSMETICS BY BOYCOTTING THE COMPANY'S PRODUCTS AND URGING OTHERS TO DO THE SAME AS THEY PROTEST AT L'ORÉAL HEADQUARTERS IN LONDON, ENGLAND.

to provide data for poison control centers and emergency room personnel to use in saving lives when products are misused.

Many laws, regulations, and guidelines govern product safety testing. They include the following:

Federal Statutes:

- **The Food, Drug, and Cosmetic Act**
- **Toxic Substances Control Act**
- **Federal Insecticide, Fungicide, and Rodenticide Act**
- **Clean Air and Water Acts**
- **Consumer Product Safety Act**

Federal Enforcement Agencies for the above laws are:

- **U.S. Food and Drug Administration (FDA)**
- **Environmental Protection Agency (EPA)**
- **Consumer Product Safety Commission (CPSC)**
- **Occupational Safety and Health Administration (OSHA)**

Chemical testing in the United States is carried out under the supervision of the National Toxicology Program (NTP). NTP oversees and coordinates chemical testing for the National Institute of Environmental Health Sciences (NIEHS), the National Institutes of Health (NIH), the Federal Drug Administration's National Center for Toxicological Research (NCTR), and the Centers for Disease Control and Prevention's National Institute for Occupational Safety and Health (NIOSH).

Government agencies have banned some substances after the NTP tested them using animals. Other substances have been restricted for use by industry after testing in animals. For example:

- **A water process has replaced methylene chloride, used to decaffeinate coffee, because water doesn't leave a harmful residue and methylene chloride, a cancer-causing chemical, can.**

- **The Food and Drug Administration has restricted or eliminated various food additives and dyes after NTP tests showed adverse effects.**

- **In 1991, the Environmental Protection Agency barred dichlorvos, a chemical used for flea collars and no-pest strips after it was found to cause cancer in animals. A 1995 study confirmed the link between dichlorvos exposure and human leukemia.**

- **Benzene, a gasoline additive, is no longer used in consumer products because of evidence it can cause cancer in humans.**

When scientists at the National Toxicology Program tested these drugs and other compounds used in large quantities, fewer than 10 percent proved carcinogenic. Substances the NTP has tested for possible carcinogenic qualities, as well as other data collected, are listed in the *Biennial Report on Carcinogens,* which is submitted to Congress and made public by the secretary of Health and Human Services.

In addition to testing substances for cancer-causing ability, NTP also does tests and collects test results on such problems as genetic and reproductive toxicity, birth defects, and impairment of the brain and nervous system.

Several incidents of products harming American consumers took place before the 1938 passage of the Food, Drug, and Cosmetic Act (FDCA). For example, in 1933, an eyelash cosmetic called Lash Lure caused allergic reactions in some women, and blinded at least one woman, but there was no federal law giving the government the authority to have the product withdrawn. In another consumer product scare in 1937, sulfanilamide, one of the first antibiotics, was mistakenly dissolved in an antifreeze solvent called diethylene glycol to make a liquid marketed as Elixir of sulfanilamide, which was supposed to help cure certain infections, especially in children. Diethylene glycol causes serious damage to the kidneys, and more than a hundred Americans, many of them children, died after taking the elixir.

After the FDCA was passed in 1938, federal law required manufacturers to be responsible for insuring the safety of their products before marketing them.

The Food and Drug Administration (FDA) enforces the FDCA. It "strongly urges" manufacturers to establish that their products are safe for human use, but it does not say that animal testing must be used. Animal testing, however, has proved to be the most effective way to demonstrate product safety. Under this act, cosmetics that have not been adequately tested for safety must be labeled: "WARNING—The safety of this product has not been determined."

The Federal Hazardous Substances Act (FHSA) covers household product safety. The Consumer Product Safety Commission enforces this act. Again, manufacturers must prove that their products are safe for human use. They are not required by law to use animal testing, but this method is most often used to certify that products are safe.

It isn't practical or desirable to use millions or even thousands of animals in chemical toxicity tests. Therefore, most tests have been performed on fifty to one hundred male and female animals in each dose group. However, scientists have drastically reduced the number of animals needed for product safety testing, and now may use just ten to twenty animals. Usually, two rodent species (rat or mouse) and one non-rodent species (cat, dog, or rabbit) are used in a single chemical study. The animals might be given varying doses of the chemical being tested over a two-year period.

The U.S. Congress, Office of Technology Assessment, has categorized the following product tests using animals:

Acute toxicity tests. Test animals are administered a single dose of a chemical at a dose capable of causing toxic effects or death. An example is the Lethal Dose 50 (LD50) test, first devised by British pharmacologist J. W. Trevan in 1927. The test determined the dose of a chemical required to kill half of the animals tested within a specified time period.

Since 1984, the EPA has discouraged the use of the LD50. Originally, the LD50 test took several days and generally used 200 or more animals. Usually, the substance was given to the animal through a tube inserted down the esophagus and into the stomach. At the end of the test period, animals that were not already dead were killed.

The LD50 test was intended to yield information on the amount of a substance that would cause harm to people, but its value has long been questioned. Although applying the data to humans was difficult, eventually the United States and several other countries accepted the LD50 test as the standard for determining chemical toxicity.

Opponents of lethal dose tests argue that results can be affected by several variables that make such tests scientifically unreliable. Variables include:

- **Age and sex of the animals tested;**
- **The test animals' housing and nutritional conditions;**
- **Temperature in the laboratory;**
- **Time of day and year;**
- **The exact method used to administer the substance.**

Different species react differently to the substances, and reactions of animals within the same species can also vary greatly. In addition, test results depend greatly on observation, and one observer might call a substance "highly toxic," while another labels it simply "slightly toxic." Others who oppose lethal dose testing do so on the grounds that it is appalling to intentionally poison animals, simply to test consumer products.

Federal agencies now suggest using a tiered testing procedure rather than the classic LD50 test. This modified test requires the review of available data on chemicals already tested or on structurally related chemicals, then the performance of a "limit" test, which uses ten to twenty animals instead of eighty to one hundred. Mice and rats are generally used, and are given a single dose of a product based on their body weight. The dosed animals are observed for abnormal behavior and are carefully watched during recovery. After a certain length of time the animals are euthanized, and autopsies are done to determine if any damage occurred to organ systems.

MOST PEOPLE INTERESTED IN THE HUMANE TREATMENT OF ANIMALS HOPE THAT ALTERNATIVES CAN BE FOUND TO THE ONE PICTURED HERE, IN WHICH RABBITS ARE BEING USED FOR PHARMACEUTICAL TESTS.

Eye and skin irritation tests. Such tests performed on rabbits also began in the 1920s. After World War I when soldiers were exposed to mustard gas, rabbits were tested to see what, if any, long-term effects were caused by the gas. Later, rabbit eye and skin irritancy tests were used to measure the harmfulness of chemicals found in household products and cosmetics. In 1944, John Draize, an American scientist who worked for the Food and Drug Administration, devised a method of scoring eye and skin irritants by using albino rabbits.

In the Draize test for eye irritancy, chemical solutions are applied directly into one eye of albino rabbits. (The other eye acts as a control.) As the test was first performed, to prevent the rabbits from clawing at their eyes, they were immobilized in restraining stocks from which only their heads protruded. The same test was used for skin irritancy by applying test chemical to the rabbits' shaved and abraded skin. This test has been widely condemned as being exceptionally inhumane.

In today's version of the Draize test, as few as three test animals are used. Rabbits are used because they are easy to handle, and their eyes are as sensitive as the human eye. When drops of a test substance are placed in animals' eyes, ophthalmic anesthetics are used whenever possible, as well as diluted solutions and lower doses. These modifications have eliminated the need to place the animals in stocks to restrain them. During the tests the rabbits can move freely and have constant access to food and water.

Despite objections that the test is inhumane, the Draize test continues to be used because, according to the Food and Drug Administration, "the Draize eye irritancy test is currently the most meaningful and reliable method for evaluating the hazard or safety of a substance introduced into or around the eye."

Other product tests that use animals include:

- **Biological screening tests. Organic compounds are administered to animals to determine what biological reactions the compounds cause.**

- **Carcinogenicity test. Animals (usually rodents) are exposed to different chemicals to determine if the chemicals cause cancer.**

- **Developmental and reproductive toxicity tests. Various chemicals are administered to test animals to see if the chemicals cause miscarriages, infertility, or birth defects in offspring. The tests are usually performed on rodents and rabbits.**

- **Mutagenicity tests are performed to see if a substance causes genetic mutations in test animals.**

- **Neurotoxicity tests are performed to see if a substance causes test animals to have neurological problems such as loss of coordination, loss of learning ability, or observable behavioral changes.**

- **Repeated dose chronic toxicity tests determine any harmful effects of substances administered, usually to rodents, over a period of time, usually two weeks to twelve months.**

In 1998, Vice President Al Gore worked with the United States Environmental Protection Agency (EPA) to create the High Production Volume Challenge (HPVC) program. As soon as the program was announced, it became a factor in the animal welfare argument.

According to the EPA, the goals of the program are to collect health and environmental information on 2,800 common chemicals and make the information available to the public. The classification "High Production Volume" for chemicals means that they are made or imported into the United States in large quantities. The HPVC program requires companies that use the chemicals to test them to check the degree of toxicity. In most cases, this is done through animal testing.

Those in favor of the HPVC program believe it will add to our knowledge of certain chemicals found in the environment. They say it will help the public better understand chemical hazards they may come in contact with in their daily lives and will lead to better health and safety.

Opponents call the HPVC program a waste of time, money, and animals' lives, since many of the chemicals, such as rat poison, turpentine, and benzene, have already been tested, and are known to be toxic. The Food and Drug Administration has already pronounced other chemicals on the list to be safe, such as caffeine and sorbitol which is found in chewing gum. Test new chemicals on the list, opponents say, but don't duplicate tests already performed, and use tests that don't require the use of animals.

What can you do if you don't want to buy products that have been tested on animals? Several animal welfare and animal rights groups maintain Web sites that can refer you to companies that claim their products are "cruelty free," or "not tested on animals." For example, All For Animals, an organization based in California, offers such a list on the group's Web site. PETA also lists companies that claim they do not test their products on animals. However, the Foundation for Biomedical Research cautions, "The term 'cruelty-free' is often misused and misunderstood. Companies that claim they conduct no animal testing either contract testing to an outside laboratory or use compounds known to be safe through previous animal testing."

5

Biomedical Research

National polls have revealed that most people are unaware of the many laws and regulations that govern the use of animals in biomedical research and in product safety testing. This makes the average person more likely to believe false charges of abuse made by those who oppose any form of animal research or testing. Scientists who work with animals must follow a comprehensive system of federal, state, and local laws and regulations. Researchers also follow guidelines issued by research organizations, such as the National Association for Biomedical Research.

In 1966, Congress passed the Laboratory Animal Welfare Act, which regulated the care and treatment of animals other than rodents and birds used in research experiments. The Animal Welfare Act (AWA), as it is now called, added protection for zoo and circus animals in 1970 and 1976. New federal rules concerning the treatment of laboratory animals were passed in 1985 when the act was again amended. The Animal Welfare Act was amended again in

Laws Governing the Use of Animals in Biomedical Research

The major laws, regulations, and guidelines that must be followed when animals are used for biomedical research include:

• *U.S. Government Principles for the Utilization and Care of Vertebrate Animals Used in Testing, Research and Training*

• Animal Welfare Act and the *U.S. Department of Agriculture Animal Welfare Regulations and Standards*

• Public Health Service Act and the U.S. Public Health Service Policy on Humane Care and Use of Laboratory Animals

• *Guide for the Care and Use of Laboratory Animals* prepared by the National Academy of Sciences Institute for Laboratory Animal Resources

• Good Laboratory Practice Standards of the Food & Drug and Environmental Protection Administrations

• Endangered Species Act

• Freedom of Information Act

1990, and is frequently updated. The act applies to all research facilities—public or private, academic, and industry-based—whether or not they receive federal funds. It is the only federal law that regulates the treatment of animals in research, exhibition, transport, and by dealers. Other United States agencies' laws, policies, and guidelines may include additional species coverage or specifications for animal care and use, but all refer to the Animal Welfare Act as the minimum acceptable standard.

The U.S. Department of Agriculture, Animal and Plant Health Inspection Service enforces the Animal Welfare Act through its Regulatory Enforcement and Animal Care (REAC) units. The act requires all laboratories using animals to register with and be inspected by the Animal and Plant Health Inspection Service. The REAC units conduct inspections of laboratories, the compilation of statistics on animal use from institutional reports, and levy sanctions against laboratories found in violation of the Animal Welfare Act. Laboratory animal veterinarians have much of the responsibility for actual laboratory implementation of federal regulations.

The 1985 amendments to the act also require each animal research institution to establish an Institutional Animal Care and Use Committee (IACUC). The committee is made up of researchers who are physicians or other scientists, and others. At least two members of the committee must

RESEARCHERS INJECT CHICKEN EGGS AT STERLING LABORATORIES IN ALBANY, NEW YORK. INJECTING CHICKEN EGGS WITH LIVE OR DEAD VIRUSES IS PART OF THE PROCESS FOR CREATING VACCINES.

not be affiliated with the institution, and one of these members must be a veterinarian. The committees must approve all experiments and are responsible for ensuring the safety and conditions of the animals in their respective institutions. The committee can terminate any research project it believes is not providing the animal care mandated by the Animal Welfare Act.

Under federal regulations, before scientists gain approval for work involving animals, they must submit an animal care and use plan to the Institutional Animal Care and Use Committee at their facility. The plan must include:

- **The reason for using animals and the species and number to be used;**

- **A complete description of the proposed use of the animals;**

- **A description of all procedures to be used. (The procedures must be designed to assure that any discomfort and pain to the animals is limited to that which is unavoidable for the validity of the research. Procedures must include provisions for the use of painkillers, anesthetics, and tranquilizers where appropriate to minimize discomfort and pain.)**

- **A description of any euthanasia method;**

- **Assurance that the proposed research does not unnecessarily duplicate previous research;**

- **Consideration of nonanimal alternatives if the proposed procedure might cause more than momentary or slight pain or distress to the animals. (If more than momentary or slight pain or distress might be caused to the animals, and no nonanimal alternatives can be found, the researcher must document his or her attempts to find nonanimal alternatives.)**

When a plan is submitted to the IACUC, the committee may approve, reject, or ask for additional information. The plan will be rejected if it does not sufficiently address each area of animal care. The researcher may resubmit a changed plan to the committee if all concerns are addressed.

Once the research project has begun, any future changes must be committee-approved, and the committee can suspend the work for cause. The committee must inspect the research institution's animal facilities at least every six months.

With each amendment of the Animal Welfare Act, REAC interprets the act's provisions and issues regulations. Among the many provisions of the act are those that:

- **Regulate conditions of the housing of primates used in research;**

- **Determine the requirements for environmental enhancement and psychological well-being of primates;**

- **Determine the primary enclosure requirements for dogs, cats, guinea pigs, hamsters, and rabbits;**

- **Regulate exercise requirements for dogs;**

- **Require record-keeping and reporting that includes the number of animals used in experiments, except mice, rats, and birds;**

- **Mandate the use of anesthetics for painful procedures, unless the purpose of the experiment would be jeopardized by the anesthetic;**

- **Require proper postoperative care of animals undergoing procedures;**

- **Mandate that animals undergo only one major procedure.**

In addition to U.S. Department of Agriculture regulations, the Public Health Service (PHS) enforces yet another layer of regulation. The Health Research Extension Act of 1985 gave the PHS the authority to draw up guidelines for all animal researchers seeking federal grants. The guidelines are published in the *Public Health Service Policy on Humane Care and Use of Laboratory Animals*. They cover all live, vertebrate animals, including rats, mice, and birds. PHS guidelines cover pre- and post-surgical care of research animals, veterinary and nursing care, and the use of analgesics, tranquilizers, and anesthetics. The Office for Protection from Research Risks (OPRR), within the PHS, located at the National Institutes of Health, implements and oversees PHS policy. The OPRR also investigates complaints of animal abuse against research scientists and laboratories.

To add to the regulations governing animal research, the PHS also follows another set of guidelines, the "U.S. Government Principles for the Utilization and Care of Vertebrate Animals Used in Research." The principles stressed in this document are humane care, reduction of pain, and species-appropriate living conditions.

A non-government laboratory organization, the Association for Assessment and Accreditation of Laboratory Animal Care International (AAALAC), also encourages the humane and appropriate treatment of laboratory animals. The organization monitors member laboratories and conducts on-site inspections.

In *The Principles of Humane Experimental Technique* (1959), W. M. S. Russell and Rex Burch introduced the concept of following the Three Rs (3Rs) for responsible animal testing—reduction, refinement, and replacement. The Animal Welfare Act incorporates the 3Rs concept and encourages scientists engaged in animal testing to:

1. *Reduce* the number of animals used. "Reduction means we predict what the data will look like," says John

Young of Americans for Medical Advancement. "Then we use the appropriate number of animals per group. We don't always necessarily use fewer animals for every experiment. In some cases, we may need more animals. Reduction simply means we use the appropriate number of animals per study."

2. *Refine* experimental techniques to minimize pain and distress in the animals. The laboratory animal veterinarian is involved in every animal study, Young emphasizes. "He or she helps to see that the animal suffers the least amount of stress possible. For example, instead of injecting a mouse with a substance every day, or several times a day for several weeks, we can implant an osmotic mini-pump that will automatically deliver a certain dose to the mouse's system at specific times. The mouse only has to undergo one invasive procedure. This is more humane, and it is better science."

3. *Replace* the use of animals with other technologies whenever possible. "Animal rights groups always want scientists to replace animals that are higher on the evolutionary scale with those with less value to society," says Young. "We can now use rodents for many procedures that used to require dogs." Sometimes alternative testing methods that do not use animals can be used, as when drugs are screened using tissue cultures.

All facilities that keep animals regulated under the Animal Welfare Act must be licensed or registered with APHIS. One-hundred-five USDA, APHIS animal care inspectors visit registered facilities throughout the United States to check for compliance with the act through annual unannounced inspections.

Scientists familiar with the scientific method and sound experiment design emphasize that animals are never used simply as "furry test tubes." Well-designed tests offer the most reliable results, emphasize Roger and Deborah Fouts and Gabriel S. Waters in "The Ethics and Efficacy of Bio-medical Research in Chimpanzees with Special Regard to HIV Research." They also help ensure that animals are not unnecessarily subjected to invasive procedures. According to the authors, some questions should be routinely addressed:

- **Were the proper sampling methods used?**

- **Did the experiment design meet all the assumptions of the statistical test used?**

- **Were any variables overlooked that could affect the outcome of the experiment?**

- **Does the experimenter's test design support the hypothesis he or she wants to test?**

While scientists who want to use animals in their research are designing a project, in order for the science to be valid they want to be sure that:

- **The potential application of the experiments has clinical importance;**

- **The review process is rigorous;**

- **Review involves the community and animal welfare people;**

- **The animal care program is methodical and thorough;**

- **The animals are not subject to pain or discomfort.**

According to Greg Popken, only a small portion—about 15 percent—of proposed research projects are approved for funding every year. This competition means that only the most valuable and well-planned projects get government funding.

The history of animal testing includes many incidents of overkill and inhumane treatment of animals, but respon-

THESE LABORATORY RATS HAVE BEEN ISOLATED IN BOTTLES FOR A METABOLISM STUDY. THEY ARE FED SUGAR AND THEN THE VOLUME OF THEIR EXHALED AIR IS MEASURED.

sible scientists now ideally strive to design experiments thoughtfully and follow the 3Rs. They treat animals used in testing humanely, design experiments appropriate for the theory being tested, and look for alternative testing methods whenever possible. "This only makes good sense," Young states, because poorly designed experiments can be canceled, and funding for a project can be withdrawn or refused. In addition, poorly designed experiments that disregard the humane care of animals used will also produce unreliable or skewed results, if such experiments can gain approval at all.

Society can only hope that those scientists who do not treat research animals humanely will be driven from the system. Seventy percent of the American public are said to support the necessary use of animals in biomedical research. Yet they also want to know that the animals are treated humanely, do not suffer, and are kept under conditions that allow them to be as healthy and comfortable as possible.

6
Using Animals in Education

Many of us have fond memories of elementary school classroom pets. They were usually goldfish or guppies, hamsters, gerbils, mice, rats, or guinea pigs, and we took turns caring for them. We might have read books about the classroom animal or written poems or stories about him or her. We learned that the animal needed the correct food for his or her species, plenty of water, a clean, warm living environment, and a way to exercise. We probably named the animal and may even have formed an attachment to him or her before we moved on to the next grade level.

The teachers who placed the animals in our classrooms hoped we also learned compassion, a respect for life, and an understanding of responsible behavior. Perhaps we even cultivated an interest in animals that would last a lifetime.

According to the Center for Laboratory Animal Welfare in Massachusetts, part of the Massachusetts Society for the Prevention of Cruelty to Animals, "Classroom pets can, in fact, help students learn far more than the habits and needs of their species. They can also help develop observation and listening skills and serve as a catalyst for math, science, language, history, and geography lessons." However, the Center for Laboratory Animal Welfare also recommends that teachers plan carefully before placing an animal in the classroom.

For example, factors that teachers and older students need to consider before keeping animals in the classroom could also apply to keeping an animal in your home:

- **Can the animal withstand variations in classroom temperature, as when thermostats are turned down at night and on the weekends?**

- **Can teachers and students adequately meet the animal's needs? (Rabbits, for instance, need to chew and should be let out of their cages for daily exercise.)**

- **Is the animal safe for children to handle? (Turtles, snakes, and lizards often carry salmonella bacteria, which can present a health risk to anyone who handles them.)**

- **Is there a local veterinarian who is knowledgeable about the species and can care for the animal if it becomes ill?**

- **Wild animals do not make good classroom pets, and there may be state laws that prevent keeping a wild animal in captivity.**

The Center for Laboratory Animal Welfare also recommends that elementary and secondary students be limited to studying the normal living patterns, behavior, development, and environmental relationships of live animals. Invasive procedures should not be attempted on live animals. For middle school and high school students, the center states: "no vertebrate animals should be used in biological or behavioral experiments that cause pain, injury, stress, or suffering, or interfere in any way with the animal's normal development, health, behavior, or environment."

For instance, the center recommends against hatching fertilized chicken eggs in the classroom because of the difficulty in meeting the requirements of egg rotation, humidity, and temperature control during and after hatching. Too many chicks are hatched ill or deformed in these situations, and it is difficult to find suitable homes for them. Chicken farms usually will not accept the chicks, and simply killing them after the exercise is completed sends the message that the animals are disposable commodities, instead of living, feeling beings.

What about dissecting animals in secondary classrooms? Many science teachers maintain that students learn anatomy-physiology best through hands-on experience, or dissection of a preserved animal, such as a cat, pig, frog, or rat. The National Science Teachers Association believes this activity is appropriate if certain guidelines are followed. According to the NSTA, laboratory and dissection activities:

- **Must be conducted with consideration and appreciation for the organism;**

- **Must be conducted in a clean and organized work space with care and laboratory precision;**

- **Must be based on carefully planned activities;**

- **Must be appropriate to maturity level of students;**

- **Must consider the student's views or beliefs. Students who are strongly against dissection should be provided with appropriate alternative activities.**

At the secondary level, dissection of preserved animals is increasingly being replaced in classrooms by studies of models, textbook illustrations, and videos that teach vertebrate anatomy-physiology.

Teachers have become increasingly aware of sending a message of concern for animals in the classroom. This has not always been true. A university biology laboratory instructor tells of collecting her own frogs in the wild in the late 1960s, when her department's budget prevented her from buying preserved specimens for dissection. (This is discouraged today, because some species of frogs and other animals are disappearing from their natural habitats.) The live frogs obtained by this laboratory instructor were "pithed"—that is, students pierced their brains with sharp needles, rendering them alive, but supposedly unable to move or feel. In this condition, beating hearts could be exposed, and muscle tissue could be stimulated with various chemicals to gauge reactions. While the exercise may have taught students some useful lessons about the anatomy-physiology of a live animal, it was understandably disturbing to many of the students who participated and sent the message that live animals are to be used as instructors see fit, with little regard for the well-being of the animals.

In his 1994 memoirs, the late Isaac Asimov, a well-known science fiction and science writer, tells another horror story about animal dissection. In 1935, he entered college in New York City at the age of fifteen and planned to pursue a zoology major. Asimov changed his mind about his major, however, when his zoology teacher told each of the students in his class to find an alley cat, kill it, and bring it to class for dissection. He managed to complete his assignment, but said in his memoirs that the experience tortured him for the rest of his life.

More recently, and in stark contrast to the above examples, a third grade teacher in New England took her students to a vacant lot near the school to look at earthworms. The students studied the earthworm's natural habitat, then, back in the classroom, discussed how they might keep the animals in the classroom. A call to the local museum of natural history confirmed that the students should be able to care for the earthworms adequately. The teacher ordered earthworms that would come with egg cases and baby worms from a biological supply house. In the meantime, the children

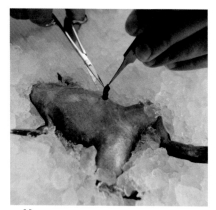

HERE, A RESEARCHER REMOVES A FROG'S INTESTINES.

prepared a terrarium to hold the worms. They placed black paper over the sides, and put soil, leaves, and grass inside.

After the earthworms arrived and were settled in their new home, the students began observing them and recording their habits. They described the worms' color and shape, and how they moved. They decided to answer a list of questions about the worms, including: How do earthworms have babies? Do earthworms like one kind of soil better than another? How do earthworms move through the ground? How big can an earthworm grow? What do earthworms like to eat?

As the students worked on answering their questions about the earthworms, they decided to place some of them in an empty ant farm with glass sides, so they could see what they did underground.

In this exercise using living animals, carefully planned by one elementary school teacher, students learned several useful lessons. They learned that:

- **Different animals have different needs;**

- **The structure and function of earthworms is distinctive from that of other animals;**

- **Earthworms behave in a distinctive manner;**

- **The earthworm's life cycle includes laying eggs that hatch into baby worms;**

- **People who keep animals must learn all about them, in order to care for them correctly and humanely.**

Sally Spear, a middle school teacher in Nashville, Tennessee, believes so firmly in the benefits of keeping classroom pets that at the beginning of the 2003 school year she had nine, including Max the ferret, Oscar the king snake, a few gerbils, a corn snake, and some bearded dragons (a type of lizard). Max, the ferret, is so hyperactive that he prefers running around the classroom to sleeping in the hammock in his cage.

Spear takes precautions each year before introducing the animals, by sending a note home with each student, asking if they have any allergies or health problems relating to animals. Spear told a reporter for *USA Today* that she takes classroom animals home if a student is allergic to animals, or has asthma-related problems with animals.

To prevent salmonella infections, Spear keeps bottles of antibacterial soap in the classroom, so that students can wash before and after handling the animals or their cages.

Despite precautions teachers may take, some organizations say animals should never be kept in the classroom. PETA opposes keeping animals in the classroom, because they are caged, and because of the danger of mishandling. "There are more constructive ways to learn about living beings than by holding them captive in hazardous and neglectful classroom settings," said Holly Quaglia, humane educator for PETA, in an October 2003 issue of *USA Today*.

The American Lung Association and the U.S. Environmental Protection Agency (EPA) do not recommend absolutely against using animals in the classroom, but both organizations caution that classroom animals should be kept away from ventilation systems and students with health problems because pet dander can trigger asthma attacks and other respiratory problems.

Some veterinary and medical schools are opting to replace the use of live animals in the classroom with studies of computer programs, plastic models of organs, and animal tissues obtained from grocery stores and slaughterhouses. The number of animals used in classroom dissection projects can also be reduced by teacher demonstrations and group projects.

Elementary and secondary teachers have recognized the need for compassion and thoughtful planning in introducing live animals to the classroom or providing preserved animal specimens for dissection. Furthermore, universities have realized that students and personnel who handle live animals need appropriate training to ensure that the animals are humanely handled and do not suffer undue pain or distress.

At the University of Wisconsin in Madison, for example, approximately 3,500 people work with laboratory animals, handling a wide variety of species. The animals range from fish to primates, but nearly 95 percent of the lab animals used at UW–Madison are rodents. The university uses about 115,000 mice and 18,000 rats annually. Federal agencies, such as the National Institutes of Health and the U.S. Department of Agriculture, fund most of the research projects at UW–Madison that use animals.

Because animals are important to many university projects, the school is careful to ensure that every person who works with a laboratory animal is providing the utmost in protective and humane care. "We don't take the use of animals lightly," says Scott Hubbard-Van Stelle, a veterinary technician, instructor at the university's Research Animal Resource Center (RARC), and animal welfare advocate. "We consider the use of animals a privilege, not a right."

The RARC at UW–Madison offers free training courses for lab animal users. The courses cover animal welfare issues, animal handling and surgical techniques, and how to use specialized equipment. They are offered to ensure that anyone whose job involves handling laboratory animals will be able to offer safe and humane animal care. An orientation course offered by the center is required for anyone on campus who handles animals or will observe animals in the classroom. "In the orientation class we talk about our philosophy concerning using animals in research and teaching. For instance, we emphasize that researchers doing surgery have to supply anesthesia and analgesia, to reduce pain and stress in the animals," says Hubbard-Van Stelle. And researchers who fill out an animal use protocol but do not have the necessary experience in handling animals are required to take further training, either from other researchers, at the RARC, or from other sources before their proposed animal research project can be approved.

The RARC also purchases and maintains equipment that can be borrowed or purchased by other laboratories. Hubbard-Van Stelle says:

> **Not every lab can afford the best equipment. Things like tabletop anesthesia units, to make life easier on the animal. If you can put an animal in a gas anesthesia chamber, it will go to sleep in a matter of seconds. You can do the procedures you need to do and then the animal wakes up very quickly. If you give injectable drugs they have to be metabolized by the body and excreted. The animals wake up much more slowly and it's much more stressful.**

In a one-day class called megasurgery, students at the RARC learn such animal-care techniques as how to hold rats to minimize stress, the different types of anesthesia, the steps involved in preparing a mouse or rat for surgery, suture types and suturing procedures, and how to avoid causing an animal pain during an injection. Students in RARC classes range from those who have never before handled an animal to participants with medical degrees. For all surgical procedures performed on living animals, the students practice sterile technique, just as a surgeon would if the patients were human, and surgical instruments and the surgical area are also sterile.

Students in the megasurgery class at RARC also practice suturing on pigs' feet donated by a local slaughterhouse. Suturing real tissue is a more accurate experience for students than using a sponge, an orange, or a banana, says Hubbard-Van Stelle.

After completing training at RARC, the students are reminded that they can ask RARC staff for help when they return to their respective jobs or courses of study. Whether it be using a piece of equipment, working on an animal, determining how much anesthesia to give, or any other animal-handling technique, RARC staff members are available for consultation.

"How people feel about using animals for research depends on their perspective," Richard Lane, associate director of the Research Animal Resource Center, told *Wisconsin Week* in May 2003. "Computer simulations and cell cultures are good, but they do not provide the complexity that living systems do." For instance, RARC students learn to remove the spleen from a living rat by actually performing the surgery. First they watch a video that details the procedure. Then they review the steps they will follow, from sterile technique, to anesthetizing the animal, to actually performing the surgery. They learn to monitor the animal during surgery to be sure all is going well, and to complete the "patient's" surgical record.

"We emphasize that these laboratory animals are living, breathing, feeling creatures," Hubbard-Van Stelle says, "and they deserve as much compassion and respect as they can get while we are using them.

"Most researchers are torn, because they know that many of the animals used will give their lives, and that does bother many people," Hubbard-Van Stelle continues. Euthanizing animals is also a concern. "When I euthanize an animal I thank the animal—literally out loud. I don't care who is around me when I do this; I thank the animal for giving its life to help us." And Hubbard-Van Stelle is not alone. "Some universities actually have a laboratory animal appreciation day, where they thank the animals for giving their lives to help us."

When Hubbard-Van Stelle is asked about the value of using animals in testing and teaching, he says, "I was diagnosed with cancer two years ago, so [biomedical research] has become important to me since that happened. It's opened my eyes in many ways."

The Research Animal Resource Center is a direct result of the many animal projects in progress at the University of Wisconsin in Madison. The center was created for administrative purposes, and to monitor protocols and regulations for handling animals, but it has evolved to include training for students and personnel in the humane treatment of research animals.

The RARC concept is relatively new, but animals have long been used to teach students everything from caring for an animal friend in elementary grades, to anatomy-physiology in high school and college. Clearly, most teachers have joined the effort to ensure that when animals are brought into the classroom they are given the respect, proper handling, and concern they deserve. In carefully conceived and humanely conducted animal studies, students of all ages can learn about an animal's life cycle, the basic needs of animals, the structures and functions of an animal, some features of animal behavior, and, most of all, a lasting respect for a nonhuman living being.

7

Animal Rights Extremists

Members of some animal rights groups are so radical in their beliefs that they are called *extremists*. Extremist groups are strongly against any animal testing or experimentation on ethical grounds, and they include many of the groups that label themselves animal *rights* organizations. People for the Ethical Treatment of Animals (PETA) and the Animal Liberation Front (ALF) are two such organizations that are often in the news. The ALF has become notorious for acts of violence and intimidation against individuals and for vandalism, theft, and arson committed against institutions using animals in any way. The ALF usually takes credit for its malicious acts. PETA, however, denies taking part in criminal activities in the name of animal rights, but they often publicize the ALF's actions.

There is some evidence that PETA has paid legal fees for the ALF members who have been arrested. An organization that provides information about funding for "radical anti-consumer organizations and activists" is ActivistCash.com. All the organizations ActivistCash.com tracks are non-profit, which means consumers can view financial transactions. In 2004, ActivistCash.com posted the following information online, as evidence that PETA provides funds for animal rights activists to pay legal fees:

> **[PETA] paid $27,000 for the legal defense of Roger Troen, who was arrested for taking part in an October 1986 burglary and arson at the University of Oregon. It gave $7,500 to Fran Stephanie Trutt, who tried to murder the president of a medical laboratory. It gave $5,000 to Josh Harper, who attacked Native Americans on a whale hunt by throwing smoke bombs, shooting flares, and spraying their faces with chemical fire extinguishers. All of these monies were paid out of tax-exempt funds, the same pot of money constantly enlarged by donations from an unsuspecting general public.**

In another incident involving an extremist animal rights group in 1999, a group called The Justice Department mailed eighty-seven threats containing razor blades to medical researchers working with primates to study new drugs. After news accounts of the threatening packages were published, PETA's Ingrid Newkirk told the media: "Perhaps the mere idea of receiving a nasty missive will allow animal researchers to empathize with their victims for the first time in their lousy careers. I find it small wonder that the laboratories aren't all burning to [the] ground. If I had more guts, I'd light a match."

Other animal rights activists have made these comments:

"If the death of one rat cured all diseases it wouldn't make any difference to me." Chris DeRose, former actor, director of Last Chance for Animals.

"To those people who say, 'My father is alive because

PROTESTORS OF THE STOP HUNTINGTON ANIMAL CRUELTY MOVEMENT OUTSIDE STEPHENS INC., ON FEBRUARY 15, 2001. STEPHENS INC. IS A U.S. COMPANY WITH A CONTROVERSIAL VIVISECTION LABORATORY.

of animal experimentation,' I say, 'Yeah, well, good for you. This dog died so your father could live.' Sorry, but I am just not behind that kind of trade-off." Bill Maher, comedian and PETA celebrity spokesperson.

"The life of an ant and that of my child should be granted equal consideration," said Michael W. Fox, veterinarian and former advisor to the Humane Society of the United States.

By their own accounts, animal rights extremists have picketed manufacturers, threatened employees of laboratories and manufacturers engaged in animal testing and the families of such employees, and have destroyed laboratories and captured or set free laboratory animals, thus slowing or halting scientific studies in progress.

In Silver Springs, Maryland, in 1981, at the Institute for Behavioral Research, Edward Taub, a physiologist, was using a procedure called deafferentation on monkeys in his attempt to prove that nerves could be regenerated, and that human stroke and head injury patients could be trained to use numb limbs as nerves healed. The monkeys' nerves to appendages were severed at the spinal cord (in a surgical procedure performed under anesthesia), causing numbness in one or more limbs. Since the animals saw the numbed arms and legs as foreign objects, they often chewed off fingers and toes. The wounded appendages were not bandaged, since bandages drew more attention to the area, thus leading to more self-injury.

Alex Pacheco, cofounder of PETA with Ingrid Newkirk, found Edward Taub's name on a list of scientists receiving government funding. Posing as a student, Pacheco volunteered to work at Taub's laboratory and chose the night shift, when few people were in the facility. Pacheco's affiliation with PETA was unknown to Taub, who trusted the young man and considered him an excellent worker. When Taub left on vacation for two weeks he gave Pacheco the keys to the lab. While Taub was gone, for some reason personnel charged with cleaning the laboratory and the monkeys' cages (who had formed friendships with Pacheco) did not show up for work. Pacheco took photographs of the monkeys in filthy cages, many with bloody wounds on their hands. A technician who had befriended Pacheco also set up a photograph depicting a monkey in a crucifixion position. The photo was later used in PETA posters as illustrative of the treatment the monkeys endured at the Silver Springs laboratory, even though the pose was contrived and had nothing to do with Taub's research work. Pacheco notified the media that the animals in the laboratory were being mistreated. He also called the police.

On September 11, 1981, the police raided the Institute for Behavioral Research and removed seventeen monkeys. (It was noted later that local television crews were inside the facility when the police arrived.) Taub was charged with seventeen counts of animal cruelty. Eleven of the counts were dismissed at trial, five ended in acquittal, and one was overturned and dismissed on appeal.

At Taub's November 1981 trial, fellow scientists and

seven veterinarians who had examined the monkeys testified that Taub's work had scientific merit and that normal,
everyday conditions in the laboratory were not substandard. Although five of the veterinarians who testified were
experts in deafferentation and supported Taub's decision
not to bandage the monkeys' appendages, two said they
believed Taub was negligent in not applying bandages.
These two veterinarians were not experts on deafferentation. Roger Galvin, the prosecuting attorney, went on to
help found the California-based Animal Legal Defense
Fund, which later began working with PETA.

Taub was convicted of one count of animal cruelty,
which was overturned in 1983 by the Maryland Court of
Appeals. The court held that Maryland's anticruelty laws
could not be enforced for federally funded scientific research.

After the police raid at the Institute for Behavioral Research, a PETA volunteer offered to care for the seventeen
monkeys police had removed in her home. When the court
ordered that the monkeys be returned to Taub, on grounds
that he owned them, they mysteriously disappeared. Only
after threats of contempt of court were leveled did they
reappear. It was then discovered that they had been on a
truck to Florida and back. Veterinarians taking care of the
monkeys after their return noted signs of severe stress.
Later, some of the monkeys used in Taub's research were
autopsied, and it was found that new neural pathways
had, indeed, been growing.

Results of the incident were twofold:

**1. Taub's research project was forcibly terminated by
adverse publicity and subsequent loss of funding, thus ensuring that no human patients would ever benefit from any
good results.**

**2. The publicity generated by PETA fueled the animal-
rights movement and made PETA a household word. (PETA
sold videotapes of the incident, titled "The Silver Springs**

Monkeys," for fifteen dollars apiece, but there was no mention of dismissal of the charges against Taub, or of his acquittal.)

An incident at the University of Pennsylvania Head Injury laboratory in 1984 also terminated a biomedical study and contributed to the animal rights movement in the United States. Thomas Gennarelli, head of the laboratory, was engaged in head injury studies using baboons. The animals were forcibly injured and then medically treated. Medical treatment of the injured animals was videotaped throughout the study—a total of some sixty hours of videotape. Through his research, Gennarelli hoped to contribute to knowledge about head injuries and strokes that would help the millions of humans who suffer from such injuries.

The head injury data went drastically wrong, however, when poorly supervised student technicians practiced improper scientific technique and gross insensitivity in handling the injured baboons, all of which was videotaped. Members of the ALF broke into the laboratory, stole six years of research data, including the videotapes, and vandalized computers and medical equipment. The ALF gave the tapes to PETA, whose members compiled a twenty-six-minute tape titled, "Unnecessary Fuss." (The title was taken from a comment made by Gennarelli after the theft of the tapes.) The damning tape showed students violating scientific and humane procedure by constantly smoking, roughly handling the injured baboons, and mocking the animals with rude comments in front of the camera.

At first the University of Pennsylvania defended Gennarelli's work and refused to close the lab. Later, the tape made by PETA was so widely circulated and had such a forceful impact on those who saw it that the NIH withdrew funding for the project. The head injury laboratory was closed. The incident was clearly an example of careless and insensitive practices in one scientific laboratory, but it tainted other scientists who were using animals in their work. Scientists familiar with Gennarelli's work, however, have maintained that it did produce useful information for treating head injuries.

In another attempt by animal rights activists to end animal-based biomedical research, on July 4, 1989, burglars broke into the laboratory of physiologist John Orem at Texas Tech University and Health Sciences Center in Lubbock, Texas. Orem was conducting sleep research that could be helpful in learning why Sudden Infant Death Syndrome (SIDS) claims the life of one baby out of one thousand births in the United States. His sleep research also held promise for discovering the cause of apnea—a dangerous condition in which breathing actually stops during sleep—and for learning why pulmonary disorders worsen during sleep. Orem was using cats in his studies. The tests involved implanting electrodes in the brains of the cats, so that electroencephalographs (brain wave measurements called EEGs) could be taken. It was necessary to fit the cats with small helmets to keep them from scratching at their heads.

Since brain tissue has no pain receptors, and the cats were anesthetized when the electrodes were implanted, the cats did not suffer pain. In fact, the cats roamed freely around the laboratory, and the technicians who worked with the cats often played with them. The cats would frequently purr while they were undergoing an EEG.

Orem had refined his investigative and data-gathering techniques to the point that he obtained meaningful information using fewer than ten cats each year. The NIH said Orem's veterinary practices were excellent, and federal inspectors consistently found his laboratory above reproach. According to John Remmers, M.D., a leading pulmonologist, Orem was the only scientist in the world studying the fundamental causes of SIDS when his research was disrupted.

The burglars who entered Orem's laboratory took some of the cats used in his study, as well as his personal records. They also spray-painted walls and destroyed equipment valued at over $50,000. The burglars who took credit for the break-in were members of the ALF. PETA held a press conference shortly after the break-in in which they showed photos of the cats wearing their helmets, and claimed that Orem had "turned cats into an appliance you could plug into a wall."

In September 1989, PETA filed a formal complaint against Orem charging him with violations of Public Health Service regulations governing research animals. The Office of Protection from Research Risks (OPRR), the branch of NIH responsible for investigating such charges, exonerated Orem. The OPRR issued a statement: "OPRR has no reason to consider further action on these allegations and considers this matter closed."

PETA ignored the findings of the OPRR and continued to use the Orem incident to its advantage. PETA urged members to write Orem at his home address, to send money for billboards displaying the cats, and to purchase a video about Orem's research that portrayed him as a scientist with a "ride on the federal grant gravy train" and an abuser of animals. Orem said he even received death threats, which have continued periodically to the present.

As of summer 2004, Orem's research with cats has continued. He describes the cats as "lovely, intelligent, living beings. They are pets, and we name them. They live long, unrestrained lives in our laboratory, and it causes me great grief when we need to euthanize one to study its brain."

Also in 1989, ALF members broke into three buildings at the University of Arizona in Tucson. They stole more than a thousand animals being used in medical studies, and caused $300,000 worth of damage by burning two research laboratories, a research center, and an off-campus office.

In January 1990, Adrian R. Morrison's laboratory at the University of Pennsylvania, School of Veterinary Medicine, was also ransacked. Morrison, D.V.M., Ph.D., was also using cats to study the brain in sleep. The intruders stole correspondence, manuscripts, grant applications, and

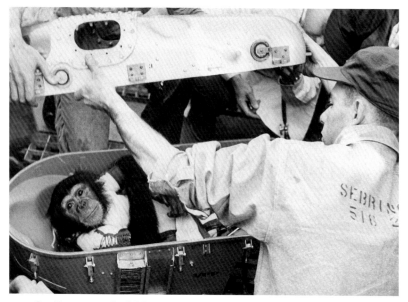

ON FEBRUARY 1, 1961, HAM THE CHIMP RETURNED AFTER HIS TRIP INTO SPACE. HAM THE CHIMP WAS USED BEFORE MEN AND WOMEN WERE SENT INTO ORBIT.

data, and spray-painted "ALF" on walls. A short time before the break-in, Morrison had spoken out against an American Anti-Vivisection Society associate's animal rights presentation for children, had defended another scientist whose laboratory was raided, and had debated a PETA representative on a radio show. He believed the raid on his lab was related to these activities. After the raid, an article about Morrison appeared in a New York weekly, *The Village Voice*. In the article, PETA's Ingrid Newkirk was quoted as saying: "PETA intends to use Morrison to persuade other vivisectors who were heartened by his strong stand on animal research that it doesn't pay off. Now the spotlight is on him, and what happens next will deter others who might want to follow in his footsteps."

Animal rights activists demonstrated against Morrison's work at the University of Pennsylvania, sent letters to his neighbors saying that he treated animals cruelly (his neighbors defended him), made threatening telephone calls, and sent hate mail to Morrison and his family.

The animal rights attacks strengthened Morrison's resolve to continue his public efforts to expose the misinformation disseminated by extremists and to inform the public about the value of animal testing.

In *Why Animal Experimentation Matters*, Morrison's essay, "Making Choices in the Laboratory," cautions that the photos certain animal rights groups use to further their causes are often staged.

A flagrant example of this was the transmission of a video, provided by PETA, which showed a tiny kitten in a research hospital at Boys Town; with a surgical wound on its head, the kitten stumbled around on a barren floor while pathetically crying for its mother. Viewers were not informed that the animals at the facility were very well cared for, that the video was set up by the undercover people filming it [who had taken the kitten from its mother], or that the Boys Town researchers who had been targeted by PETA were a highly respected, caring husband-and-wife team.

Kittens were important to their research into causes of defective development of the hearing apparatus in the human fetus, because similar developmental stages appear in kittens.

As a result of more than a hundred such attacks on biomedical research laboratories, the Federal Bureau of Investigation now lists the ALF as a domestic terrorist organization. Without participating directly, PETA provides support and publicity for the ALF's criminal activities by making pleas for donations for legal defense funds, displaying photos of "rescued" animals in PETA publications, and encouraging supporters to take in captured animals.

The Debate
Goes On

The publicity given the incidents described in Chapter 7 helped give rise to many new animal rights groups, including but not limited to Animal Rights Mobilization, Farm Animal Reform Movement (FARM), Feminists for Animal Rights, Mobilization for Animals, and In Defense of Animals. By 1994, there were about 400 animal advocacy groups in the United States, with a combined total income of $50 million. In June 2004, the World Animal Net Directory listed 15,000 organizations classified as "animal protection societies." The estimated total income of the top fifteen animal extremist organizations in 2003 was $130 million. By comparison, the combined 2003 budget of the three main national pro-animal testing groups—Americans for Medical Advancement, the National Association for Biomedical Research, and the Foundation for Biomedical Research—was just $4 million, and, that figure includes budgets for the national organizations' state affiliates.

While many aspects of the Silver Springs incident seemed contrived to generate publicity for the animal rights cause, people were appalled by the media accounts and were clearly willing to contribute to the cause to help prevent animal abuse.

When extremists learn of a disreputable laboratory, or hear one of the circulating horror stories of animal abuse, they make sure that the media is informed. As a result, many members of the general public mistakenly conclude that all scientists are heartless individuals who torture animals. In fact, proponents of animal tests have claimed that animal rights extremists are adept at issuing simple statements about animal cruelty that inflame the public, while scientists attempting to explain that their work is humane and necessary often find that complicated scientific explanations go unheard.

In *Targeted: The Anatomy of an Animal Rights Attack,* authors Lorenz Otto Lutherer and Margaret Sheffield Simon, explain why it is often difficult for scientists to counter the arguments against animal testing presented by animal rights groups:

> **The scientific community has had a misconception about the scientific literacy and sophistication of the general public. When those working with animals found themselves the target of an attack [by animal rights proponents] and were forced to deal with the growth of the movement, they often resorted to sophisticated scientific explanations which were interpreted as evasive or even arrogant by those who were sympathetic to the movement. . . .Those involved in the advance of biomedical and scientific progress had not stopped to consider that the mainstream of society did not understand**

the fundamental tenets of their profession: that basic research leads to an advance of scientific knowledge which, in turn, leads to applied research that improves the human and animal condition. At the same time, they also had not faced a growing public relations problem of increased health care costs coupled with the public perception that taxpayers' money was being wasted on unnecessary and duplicative research.

During the 1980s alone, animal extremist raids did more than $10 million in damage to American institutions, laboratories, and corporations. In addition, the raids stopped or delayed research on SIDS, infant blindness, cancer, AIDS, and many other diseases and conditions that affect both people and animals. And the siege continues.

According to the Foundation for Biomedical Research, the FBI estimates that the ALF and its sister organization, the Earth Liberation Front (ELF) have committed more than six hundred criminal acts in the United States since 1996, resulting in damages in excess of $43 million.

A splinter group of the ALF, called Stop Huntingdon Animal Cruelty (SHAC) has been especially active in trying to shut down Huntingdon Life Sciences, a company based in Great Britain that uses rats, mice, dogs, and other animals to test pharmaceuticals. Employees of Huntingdon's New Jersey facility have been beaten and threatened, their cars have been vandalized and firebombed, and their homes have been vandalized.

In July 2002, Brian Cass, managing director of Huntingdon's New Jersey office, was beaten outside his home, and his colleague, who refused to be named for fear that his family would suffer, was temporarily blinded. Kevin Kjonaas, leader of the New Jersey-based chapter of SHAC, whose members allegedly committed the illegal acts against Huntingdon employees, told the media after the attack: "If a car being blown up in a driveway or animals being liberated from a lab scares them, then I would say that fear pales by comparison to the fear that the animals have every day. The kind of true violence that these animals endure at the hands of people at Huntingdon leaves me with little sympathy."

The Foundation for Biomedical Research has compiled a list documenting the worldwide criminal acts of the ALF, the ELF, and SHAC, from 1981 to the present. Here are a few of the acts committed in the United States most recently:

4/20/04: The ALF claimed credit for breaking into a pharmaceutical company in Long Island and stealing documents, other data, and building plans for a new facility.

4/15/04: Santa Fe, New Mexico—ELF members break into an SUV dealership and vandalize a 2003 Hummer, causing over $1,000 in damage.

4/9–10/04: The ALF takes credit for stealing animals from a vocational high school in Philadelphia. The animals were not used for experiments, but were cared for by students learning responsibility. The ALF left a message: "Experiment on yourselves. . . . We're free—The Animals."

3/29/04: At a pharmaceutical company in Portland, Oregon, SHAC activists pour red paint over an office and equipment, because the company did business with contract lab services.

3/1/04: Employees of the telephone company for HLS have their homes and offices vandalized, and their personal and business information is posted on the Internet.

"Criminal Acts in the Name of Animal Rights"

"Violent and Illegal Activity by Animal Activists Is Escalating," warns the Foundation for Biomedical Research. "Although animal activists portray themselves as kind and compassionate, the animal rights movement sponsors and perpetrates illegal and violent activity and these criminal acts are escalating in frequency and destructiveness."

The following graph, prepared by the Foundation for Biomedical Research, shows a sharp increase in the number of criminal acts committed in the United States in the name of animal rights, over designated five year periods.

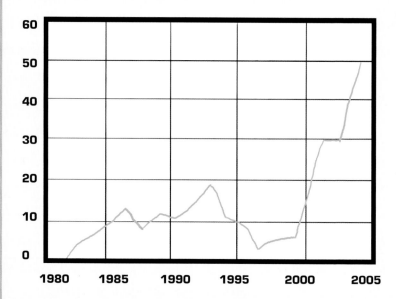

'Letter to the NIH'

On June 12, 2002, Frankie L. Trull, President of the Foundation for Biomedical Research, sent this letter about Michael Podell's announcement that he would discontinue his NIH-funded HIV research at Ohio State University to the National Institutes of Health and other government agencies:

"We are deeply concerned about the recent decision by Dr. Michael Podell to discontinue his NIH-funded research at Ohio State University. It is well known that this critical study of the effect of methamphetamine drugs on HIV-infected people has been subject to a steady and often violent campaign of harassment against Dr. Podell, his family and Ohio State University veterinary school since the NIH grant was announced in October 2000. . . .

"We are alarmed that a small, vocal, and often violent segment of the animal rights movement, rather than the scientific research community, is increasingly being allowed to define the parameters of medical research expertise. Too much is at stake to allow this to continue. We fear that the loss of Dr. Podell and his research project is merely the beginning of an ever-escalating campaign against research discovery and medical advancement.

"On behalf of FBR's broad-based scientific constituency, we urge you to provide the leadership necessary to protect biomedical research, educate the public and decision-makers of its value to all Americans and counter the inaccurate claims and destructive tactics of the animal rights movement. Please promote biomedical research and end the intimidation of our nation's medical researchers.

"We are anxious to hear NIH's response to this growing crisis in the medical research community."

Biomedical researchers engaged in animal research continue to hope that law enforcement will protect their work. The Animal Enterprise Protection Act of 1992 makes it a federal crime to travel:

> **in interstate or foreign commerce, or use or cause to be used the mail or any facility in interstate or foreign commerce, for the purpose of causing physical disruption to the functioning of an animal enterprise; and intentionally cause physical disruption to the functioning of an animal enterprise by intentionally stealing, damaging, or causing the loss of, any property (including animals or records) used by the animal enterprise, and thereby cause economic damage exceeding $10,000 to that enterprise, or conspire to do so.**

Violators of this law "shall be fined under this title or imprisoned not more than one year, or both." The law provides for harsher penalties for offenders who cause bodily harm or death, and also mandates retribution for some losses caused by offenders.

While this law would seem to be an answer to the destruction of research facilities or other enterprises involving animals, as of 2001, just one person had been prosecuted under the law. According to some sources, the law has probably not been vigorously enforced because the government has not wanted to devote resources to pursuing animal rights advocates who, in most cases, target facilities, rather than people. (The firefighters who respond to arson and bomb explosions, however, and any people who might be in the vicinity, are endangered by the acts of animal rights extremists.) Others believe the law should be enforced to the fullest, to send a message to animal rights extremists that criminal acts will not be tolerated.

Although some animal rights extremists have committed criminal acts to draw attention to their cause, most animal welfare groups continue to advocate for animals without breaking the law.

Most of those who contribute money to animal welfare and animal rights organizations do so because they hope to help animals. But any potential contributor would do well to determine the answers to these questions before sending hard-earned cash or donating time or supplies:

Does the group seem to use fund-raising as its primary activity? Most nonprofit organizations must list funds collected and expenses. What proportion of funds collected were spent for fund-raising and how much for helping animals, such as contributing to a primate retirement center or donating funds for the operation of the local pound?

Has the group's name been associated with acts of vandalism or other illegal activities, or with any incident that could be classified as domestic terrorism? An Internet search of a group's name will lead to articles mentioning the group, its accomplishments, and any illegal activities. (Web sites for organizations, understandably, will mention goals and news favorable to the organization, but will not give reports of antisocial or other negative activities.)

Where do the photos come from that are used by certain groups in brochures, or on posters or other publicity materials? Some groups have been accused of using dated photos—taken before present animal welfare laws were in place—and of staging photos for the greatest impact.

When a group claims to have "rescued" animals from a biomedical facility, what happens to those animals? (In some cases animals taken from poultry facilities or biomedical laboratories were euthanized, because the "rescuers" had no place to keep them or no way to provide the care the animals needed.)

What activities or facilities dedicated to animal welfare has the group financially supported? For instance, some groups have contributed to the placement of retired primates or have found homes for needy animals, while other groups boast of acts of vandalism, or paying the legal fees of individuals arrested for breaking into biomedical facilities.

When animal rights extremists sensationalize a biomedical study as inhumane or unnecessary, what are the facts? Did the accused facility actually violate Animal Welfare Act provisions and/or other federal and state animal welfare regulations? Or were allegations contrived and simply used to discredit a scientist's animal research project?

When you telephone group offices or headquarters for an animal welfare organization and ask how you can help, do group representatives simply ask for money, or are there other ways you can be of service, such as feeding animals or cleaning animal areas at a group's animal rescue facility? Furthermore, if you volunteer your time to the group, how will your services be used? That is, will you help care for animals in a facility, or will your services be primarily directed toward fund-raising?

When you visit animal rescue facilities sponsored by certain groups, are they practicing what they preach, or are the facilities substandard?

Does a group call itself an animal *welfare* organization (animals should be given consideration, but human needs have priority) or an animal *rights* group (humans have no authority over animals)? Animal rights groups are sometimes made up of extremists who condone illegal activities to further their cause.

Is a group disseminating misinformation about the history of biomedical research and the use of animals? Read several sources on the subject before you decide that animals have not helped scientists in their quest for better living conditions or improved health for both humans and animals. Most scientists have published articles about their work in scientific journals, and many will discuss their work with interested parties.

Also, give the scientific community its due by speaking with scientists engaged in animal research. Visit an animal laboratory that admits interested members of the public. Attend talks by biomedical researchers. Many scientists are now speaking at schools, or holding question-and-answer sessions to help inform the public about their work and the benefits realized to human and animal health from animal testing. In fact, all of the scientists quoted in this text, including John Young at Cedars-Sinai Medical Center, B. Taylor Bennett at the University of Illinois, Greg Popken at the University of North Carolina, and Scott Hubbard-Van Stelle at the University of Wisconsin–Madison, have conducted student tours through their laboratories, and have spoken to high school and college students about their work. (After a recent speech about his work, John Orem of Texas Tech University approached PETA picketers outside and invited them to visit his laboratory. "Come to Lubbock," he said, "and I'll show you what you think is so terrible.") Nobody took him up on the offer.

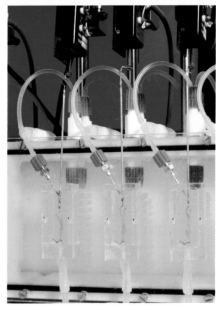

HERE, DRUG RESEARCH IS DONE ON HUMAN, RATHER THAN ANIMAL, TISSUE.

Most animal welfare advocates are sincere in their desire to help animals. They pursue their goals reasonably and nonviolently, and many believe that animal testing and biomedical research using animals is still necessary for human and animal health.

Most scientists contend that animal testing and experimentation is still vital to human survival, but they continue to work on improving tests, so that alternatives can be used increasingly, without unnecessarily sacrificing animals or losing the benefits derived from testing and scientific projects. For example, Alan Goldberg, director of the Center for Development of Alternatives to Animal Testing at Johns Hopkins University, wrote in the *Johns Hopkins Gazette*, September 10, 2001: "We have always said animals are necessary for research, and that their use is going to continue to be necessary for the foreseeable future, even with alternatives."

9

Alternatives to
Animal Testing

While it is true that scientists continue to look for alternatives to using live animals for their work, it may not be true, as some animal rights extremists claim, that alternatives are always available if scientists would just use them. For example, as stated by the National Association for Biomedical Research concerning product testing:

Scientists have significantly reduced the number of animals used in product safety testing in recent times. Because this reduction has been possible, animal rights activists would like the public to believe that the use of laboratory animals can be eliminated in this field altogether. It is often claimed that valid alternatives to the use of animal tests already exist to evaluate product safety. This is not true . . .

The fact that a given product may not require additional animal tests does not mean that testing can be abandoned for all products. New chemicals, new uses of old chemicals and new mixtures of chemicals must be subjected to toxicity testing so that unsafe products will not be marketed inadvertently.

IN A LABORATORY, SCIENTISTS PERFORM A RETINAL TRANSPLANT.

According to the Food and Drug Administration (FDA): "many procedures intended to replace animal tests are still in various states of development. . . . While the best means may begin with valuable adjunct [additional] tests, ultimately testing must progress to a whole intact, living system—an animal."

The Johns Hopkins University Center for Development of Alternatives to Animal Testing was established in 1981 to help the scientific community develop research and testing projects that use fewer animals than in the past, or that use no animals at all. Reduction, replacement, and refinement (3Rs) have been important goals for reducing the numbers of animals used in testing and experimentation. Replacement is the concept most often thought of when "alternatives to animal testing" are mentioned. If animals are no longer used at all, or if human cells or tissues are used, this is called *absolute* replacement. If animal cells or tissues are used, but not whole animals, this is called *relative* replacement. Using animal cells or tissues means that living animals are not kept in the laboratory, but often the animals are killed to obtain the cells or tissues.

Although scientists are continually searching for alternative methods for animal testing, replacement of animals is not always an option. Some kinds of testing still require the use of a living animal. For example, Texas Tech University's John Orem wants to know what happens to various human bodily functions during sleep. "There is no problem that doesn't get worse during sleep," he claims, and the cats he uses as study subjects are vital to his research. The only way to thoroughly study the subject is with animals, he says. "I can't study sleep in a dish."

Scientists use alternatives whenever possible, says Bennett, laboratory veterinarian for the University of Illinois. "In some cases, the use of alternatives has drastically reduced the number of animals used. But at some point [scientists] have to see how a compound is going to affect a system with multiple organ systems. In many cases, it's not the test compound itself that's going to react inside a living system—it's the metabolite, as the compound is broken down in the body. . . . You can't [artificially] model a system as complicated as the human body and how it reacts to a new and unused compound. I don't see how animals can ever be replaced entirely in biomedical research."

Under the 3Rs principle, however, in many cases the number of animals used has been greatly reduced, and tests have been refined to cause less pain and distress to any animals used.

One example of a test that has been refined to require fewer animals is the pregnancy test. Not long ago, if a woman wanted to know if she was pregnant she would have to visit her doctor and have a test that involved killing a rabbit. Since the 1990s, however, pregnancy tests have been sold over the counter. They are simple to use, do-it-yourself tests that detect certain chemicals in the urine that are produced during pregnancy. Animals have not been entirely eliminated from the process, however. According to Cedars-Sinai Medical Center laboratory veterinarian John Young, the antibodies used in the latest pregnancy tests are produced in animals. Young lists other alternative tests that continue to use animals in some way:

The LAL—Limulus amoebocyte lysate test. This test detects certain bacterial endotoxins in a patient's blood. A patient's blood is exposed to the blood of a horseshoe crab; a clot forms if the test is positive. The test previously used rabbits.

The LD50 test used in poison control tests is now the LD20. Scientists have increased the power of the test, but decreased the number of animals used.

The HET-CAM test uses chicken eggs to test for eye irritancy and is an alternative to the Draize rabbit eye test. The test is conducted in vitro, and the chicken embryos used in the test are destroyed.

Other alternative tests for eye irritancy include the use of donated human corneas and eyes from slaughtered cows.

The Ames test, named for its creator, Bruce Ames, uses Salmonella typhimurium. The bacteria are grown in a medium containing rat liver enzymes to test chemicals to see if they cause genetic mutations or cancer. The in vitro results are tested in a transgenic mouse called Big Blue by Stratagene, the biotech company that created the mouse. The test has not eliminated the need for animals, but has reduced the number of rodents needed.

Quantitative Structure-Activity Relationships (QSARS) is a test for chemicals. It uses a computer model that correlates the molecular structures of chemicals of known activity. In order to relate test results to human metabolism, the test requires verification in laboratory animals.

Other tests developed as alternatives to animal testing include:

Eytex: Produced by the National Testing Corp. in Palm Springs, California, Eytex is an in vitro procedure that measures eye irritancy via a protein alteration system. A vegetable protein from the jack bean mimics the reaction of the cornea to an alien substance. When a chemical is introduced, degree of irritancy is measured by cloudiness of the protein. Avon cosmetic company advertises that they use this alternative instead of the Draize eye irritancy test.

Skintex: Skintex is an in vitro method to assess skin irritancy that uses pumpkin rind to mimic the reaction of a foreign substance on human skin. Both Eytex and Skintex can measure 5,000 different materials.

Several companies have developed artificial skin systems for testing irritancy. An artificial base is seeded with live skin cells that multiply and can be useful in some tests for skin irritancy.

EpiPack and EpiSkin: Produced by Clonetics in San Diego, California, the EpiPack uses cloned human tissue to test potentially harmful substances.

Neutral Red Bioassay: Developed at Rockefeller University and promoted by Clonetics, the Neutral Red Bioassay are cultured human cells that are used to compute the absorption of a water-soluble dye to measure relative toxicity.

Test Skin: Produced by Organogenesis in Cambridge, Massachusetts, Test Skin uses human skin grown in a sterile plastic bag and can be used for measuring irritancy, etc. (this method is used by Avon, Amway, and Estee Lauder).

TOPKAT: Produced by Health Design, Inc. in Rochester, New York, TOPKAT is a computer software program that allows chemical testing based solely on a chemical's molecular structure. If the molecular structure of a new chemical is similar to a known toxic chemical, it determines that the new chemical is also toxic, without unnecessary testing on an animal. The test measures toxicity, mutagenicity (the potential to cause genetic mutations), carcinogenicity (the potential to cause cancer), and teratonogenicity (the potential to cause developmental malformations). The U.S. Army, the Environmental Protection Agency, and the U.S. Food and Drug Administration use this method.

Agarose Diffusion Method: This tests measures toxicity of plastic and synthetic devices used in medical devices such as heart valves, artificial joints, and intravenous lines. Human cells and the test material are placed in a flask and are separated by a thin-layer of agarose (a derivative of seaweed). If the material tested is an irritant, an area of killed cells appears around the substance.

Furthermore, several major federal regulatory agencies including the Environmental Protection Agency, the Occupational Safety and Health Administration, the Consumer Product Safety Commission, and the U.S. Food and Drug Administration, have agreed to accept chemical safety data from a synthetic skin test instead of an animal test—the first such substitution for live-animal tests. In the new test, developed in 2000 under the trade name Corrositex®, a chemical or chemical mixture is placed on a collagen matrix barrier that serves as a kind of synthetic skin. Corrositex® can replace, in many uses, a method in which the chemical or chemical mixture is applied to the intact skin of a laboratory animal.

Skin corrosiveness testing is conducted to ensure that chemicals and products are properly labeled to alert consumers and workers to take precautions to prevent chemical burns to the skin. Corrosion is more serious than skin irritation and involves permanent damage to skin, usually with scarring.

William Stokes, D.V.M., the National Institute of Environmental Health Sciences' (NIEHS) associate director for animal and alternative resources, said in a March 21, 2000 National Institute of Environmental Health Sciences press release, "The old test requirements called for three animals for each chemical that is evaluated for skin corrosivity and dermal irritation. Since there are more than two thousand chemicals introduced each year, the substitution of Corrositex could save many laboratory animals in a year."

An October 3, 2001, NIEHS press release noted even more progress in reducing the number of animals used in toxicity testing: "U.S. scientists are reducing the number of rodents in chemical safety testing to a fraction of the 50 to

200 animals used in the old LD50 test for toxicity, but the use of human or animal cell lines could immediately reduce the number of animals further—as much as 30 percent more."

The old LD50 test (which stands for lethal dose 50 percent) rated the toxicity of chemicals by finding the dose that killed half the test animals. Thanks to three more humane alternatives, only eight to twelve rodents are needed to estimate the lethal dose. The tests at issue determine if a chemical or product will cause illness or death in animals after ingestion of a single dose. Restrictions, warning labels, and special packaging, such as child-proof containers, are based on the results.

"The two new reports suggest that cell lines may eventually replace much animal testing but that even today cells (which are grown in cultures and reproduce indefinitely) can be used to screen chemicals for their relative toxicity, thereby further reducing the need for animals by nearly a third, the NIEHS report said.

"The reports say effective testing—including some requiring animals—remains necessary to reduce the risks of death, disfigurement and injury facing adults and children from chemicals in the workplace and in the home."

Several journals are published to keep track of alternative testing methods as they are developed. Online journals for alternatives to animal testing and experimentation include:

- *AATEX (Alternatives to Animal Testing and Experimentation)*
- *Alternatives to Animal Testing*
- *ALTEX (Alternatives to Animal Experiments)*
- *Animal Welfare*
- *ATLA (Alternatives to Laboratory Animals)*
- *In Vitro Animal*
- *Journal of Applied Animal Welfare Science*
- *Laboratory Animals*
- *Toxicology In Vitro*

Clearly, the scientific community and governments around the world are making progress in their efforts to develop alternative methods to animal testing. The day has not yet arrived when no animals are used in testing, but advances in technology may make that goal achievable in the future.

As a field called molecular toxicology progresses, biomedical research may soon enter a new era, where technology will lead to testing methods that predict reactions at a molecular level, and researchers will no longer rely on whole-animal testing results.

Technological advances in gene research may also lead to using fewer animals for research. "With the new microprocessors we can now screen 10,000 genes at a time," says Greg Popken of the University of North Carolina. (The process is called gene chip technology.) "We can use computer models to confirm a theory, but we still need whole organisms to study."

In contrast, in *What Will We Do If We Don't Experiment on Animals?* authors Ray and Jean Greek explain why studying human disease at the genetic level should lead to the abandonment of animal studies:

> **Today, technology enables us to study human disease at the genetic level—precisely where species differentiation is most pronounced, making animal-modeled research hopelessly outdated. Even genetically engineered animals, for example, knockout mice that have had one or more of their genes removed to create a specific defect, and transgenic animals, which carry genes from another species— have failed to shed new light on human disease. Why? Because changing one or two genes out of 30,000 will not make a human out of a mouse. (The genes will interact with the mouse's other 30,000 genes and behave in a completely different way from how they perform in their natural human environment.)**

According to the Greeks, a program just begun—The Human Proteome Project—will be to the study of proteins what the Human Genome Project was to the study of genes. The Human Genome Project catalogued the genes on human chromosomes, and The Human Proteome Project will catalogue all the proteins in the human body. Since genes regulate the production of proteins in the body, the study of proteins (proteomics) will add to the body of knowledge about genes, how they control protein manufacture, and how proteins affect the disease/health state in humans. This knowledge is far more valuable than analyzing animal genes and proteins, say the Greeks, and may eventually make animal experimentation unnecessary.

10
The Future of
Animal Testing

No one who loves and respects animals can dispute the fact that animals deserve to be treated humanely. Whether they exist in the wild or are pets in a household, subjects in a research laboratory, residents of an animal pound, or destined to be slaughtered for food, most people would agree that animals should never be made to suffer unnecessarily. Groups formed to advocate for the humane treatment of animals serve a worthy cause, and they have helped influence lawmakers to pass legislation that protects animals.

Animal welfare laws passed in the United States have resulted in guidelines for the treatment of animal subjects and a reduction in the total numbers of animals used. But until suitable alternatives to living animal systems have been developed as research models for humans—some scientists say this is perhaps an unachievable goal—animals will probably continue to be used to further the cause of biomedical and consumer safety research.

While developing alternative tests to animal testing is progressing steadily, animal welfare advocates have been impatient with the pace. Factors causing delays include, but are not limited to:

• **The truism, "You can't teach an old dog new tricks."** Scientists who have had success using live animals in their research projects, and who have perhaps made a name for themselves in their respective fields, may be reluctant to give up methods that have worked well for them in the past.

• **Clashes among political, scientific, and consumer groups.** Often, compromises must be worked out between the political factions that may or may not want new legislation governing animal testing, scientists who want to be relatively unhampered by government regulations in their work, and consumers who demand safe new drugs or products for personal and household use.

• **Government regulations.** Government regulations in place most often do not require alternative testing and, in fact, may mandate animal testing before a new product or drug is brought to market. Furthermore, product manufacturers fear lawsuits to the extent that they are hesitant to move away from old animal-testing practices that can serve as a defense in a civil suit, when they must show how they "proved" the product was safe before they marketed it to the public.

• **Lack of a "gold standard"** for comparing the effectiveness of alternative tests and projected results in humans. Since predicting human safety is the objective in most testing, the most accurate standard of comparison would be to compare results of human exposure to toxins with results gained through alternative testing. This is seldom possible, since there are ethical and legal barriers in place to prevent testing in humans. The best alternative has been animal testing, even though animal reactions to toxic agents are not always the same as in humans. As Martin L. Stephens, vice president for animal research issues at The Humane Society of the United States says in "An Overview of Animal Testing Issues": "Consequently, the animal test itself is typically used as the default standard against which the alternative test is judged. In other words, the lack of a true gold standard means that in vitro tests are judged by how well they accord with animal data, not human data. This 'stacks the deck' in favor of animal tests."

Greg Popken of the University of North Carolina adds another factor to the list of those factors that contribute to delays in developing alternatives to animal testing: "In many cases it just isn't technologically feasible to model many of the aspects of a living organism, much less the whole organism. . . . If we knew enough to program a computer to model the whole animal, we wouldn't have to do the research."

Despite these hindrances, however, United States and European governments are moving toward embracing those alternative tests that have proved successful.

Ray and Jean Greek have written that technology— not animal experimentation—is the answer to studying human health and disease in the future. For example:

- **Nanotechnology—the study of individual atoms—may make it possible to construct devices so tiny they can be implanted in cells to change DNA, destroy harmful bacteria, or otherwise correct problems. (A swallowable "pill" containing a tiny camera has been developed but not yet approved for human use. It will travel through patients' intestines, taking two pictures per second as it moves through the body.)**

- **A Virtual Human Being, now under construction inside computers at Oak Ridge National Laboratory in Tennessee, will react exactly as living human beings react to disease, injury, and other harmful states. The Virtual Human Being, however, will "live" entirely inside computers, where testing and experimentation can be done with keyboard strokes and mouse clicks, instead of with animal experimentation.**

- **Human volunteers can be used, in some instances, to explore conditions now studied in animals. For example, PET (positron emission tomography) and MRI (magnetic resonance imaging) are noninvasive methods for studying human brain** activity and bodily processes that could be used more extensively in research.

Focus on the further development of technology, the Greeks urge, and divert funds to that area, instead of continuing to support animal experimentation, and the future will be brighter for human and animal health.

Mahatma Gandhi, the East Indian leader who advocated for peaceful change in the laws of his country, once said, "You must be the change you wish to see in the world." The Humane Society of the United States (HSUS) uses Gandhi's words at the beginning of "42 Ways to Help Animals in Laboratories." Both HSUS and PETA urge those interested in animal welfare to follow Gandhi's example by taking part in nonviolent demonstrations on behalf of animals.

Anything kids can do peacefully to call attention to these issues is helpful. PETA's Lisa Lange says:

> They are the decisionmakers of the future and there's no stronger voice than a young person who is standing up for what [he or she] believes is right. We have a long history of people doing sit-ins and marches for various causes. [Such activities] are attention-getting and smart, and we would have a much improved world if we had young people participating in more activities like that.

True to Gandi's philosophy, in "42 Ways to Help Laboratory Animals," the Humane Society of the United States advises that nonviolent demonstrations can be a productive way to advocate for animal welfare:

> Carrying placards and chanting slogans are essential, but there are other activities that can enhance the effectiveness of a demonstration. Give speeches, unfurl a banner, perform street theater, light candles

and hold a silent vigil, sing, hand out literature, or so-
licit supportive honks from passing vehicles. Be cre-
ative and draw a crowd, but avoid shock tactics that
might offend public sensitivities and turn people off
to your cause.

In "42 Ways to Help Animals in Laboratories," the
HSUS acknowledges progress toward improving animal
welfare, such as the passage of the Animal Welfare Act and
scientists' concerned attempt to follow the 3Rs, but says
there is still work to be done. The following recommenda-
tion for becoming involved in animal welfare causes are
adopted from the HSUS publication:

1. **Live by example. Show your concern for animals in ways that
others will want to emulate—wear a button, shop for cosmetics and household products claiming not to use animals in testing, join a group that shares your goals for animal welfare.**

2. **To become a credible animal welfare advocate, do your
homework on animal welfare issues. Research both sides
in libraries, on the Web, and by speaking to scientists in
animal laboratories and to animal rights representatives.
When you have facts and statistics for both sides, you are
more likely to be heard.**

3. **Get a job with an animal protection organization in your city.**

4. **Follow your conscience in school by choosing an alternative
activity over dissecting an animal. In 2004, ten states—California, Florida, Illinois, Louisiana, Maine, Maryland, New York,
Pennsylvania, Rhode Island, and Virginia—had legislated that
such an option be available to students, and many school dis-
tricts offer such alternatives. If a teacher in your school ex-
pects students to dissect an animal and you strongly object,
ask if you can do an alternative project. HSUS has free loan
materials available for educators, including CD-ROMs, videos,**

and charts depicting animal anatomy. In addition, there are Web sites where you can dissect virtual animals, such as http://www.itg.lbl.gov/ITG.hm.pg.docs/dissect/info.html, where you can dissect a frog.

5. **Choose goals for animal welfare that you can achieve.** For instance, you might persuade a teacher to provide alternatives to animal dissection for those students who don't want to dissect an animal, but it's unlikely you can persuade the NIH to withdraw all funding for animal testing and experimentation within the next year.

6. **Accept partial victories when they are offered.** If, for example, a local university agrees to significantly reduce the number of animals used in its laboratories, but not to stop using animals entirely, that's a victory worth celebrating.

7. **Write letters to the heads of corporations, research laboratories, scientists, university presidents, or government agencies involved in animal research, politely and earnestly state your concerns about animal use. But do your homework first, and ask for improvements in specific areas**—such as reducing the number of animals used, or asking if alternative methods are used whenever possible.

8. **Circulate petitions for an animal welfare organization** that advocates working within the system for change, and sign those that favor measures you approve of for improving animal welfare.

9. **If there is no local group for animal advocacy in your area, start your own**—HSUS can tell you how.

10. **Write letters and make telephone calls to elected representatives whenever animal welfare issues are coming up for a vote,** or just to express your opinion on such issues as pound seizure.

Every day more new diseases erupt in various parts of the world, more new chemicals are provided for human use and consumption, and new medical discoveries are made. Until technology completely replaces animal models in testing and biomedical research, difficult questions remain. Should humans have the right, or do they have an obligation, to use nonhuman animals to improve human health and well-being? Do you believe technology can serve science more effectively than using animals for testing and experimentation? Is funding part of the reasoning behind animal experimentation? Where do you stand?

Notes

Foreword

p. 7, The Children's Hospital of Philadelphia. "Vaccine Education," http://www.chop.edu/consumer/jsp/microsite/microsite.jsp?id=75918 (accessed July 12, 2004).

pp. 8–9, American Academy of Pediatrics, "When Do Children and Teens Need Vaccinations?" http://www.cispimmunize.org/ (accessed July 12, 2004).

p. 11, The Associated Press, "Virus Experiment in Mice Could be First Step Toward a Vaccine," *USA Today*, p. 7D, August 12, 2003.

pp. 11–12, Reuters News Service, "New SARS Vaccine Shows Promising Results," June 24, 2004: http://msnbc.msn.com/id/5282050/ (accessed July 12, 2004).

Chapter 1

p. 14, Greek, C. Ray, M.D., and Jean Swingle Greek, D.V.M., *Sacred Cows and Golden Geese: The Human Cost of Experiments on Animals* (New York: Continuum, 2000), p. 23.

p. 15, Monamy, Vaughn. *Animal Experimentation: A Guide to the Issues* (Cambridge, United Kingdom: Cambridge University Press), 2000, p. 11.

pp. 16–17, Monamy, p. 12.

pp. 18–19, Francis ed., *Life and Letters of Charles Darwin*, (New York: Basic Books, 1959), pp. 382–383.

p. 21, Rudacille, Deborah. *The Scalpel and the Butterfly: The War Between Animal Research and Animal Protection* (New York: Farrar, Straus and Giroux, 2000), p. 28.

p. 22, Paul, Ellen Frankel, and Jeffrey Paul, *Why Animal Experimentation Matters: The Use of Animals in Medical Research* (New Brunswick, NJ: Transaction Publishers 2001), pp. 7–8.

p. 24, Monamy, Vaughn. *Animal Experimentation*, p. 32.

pp. 27–28, Paul and Paul, *Why Animal Experimentation Matters*, pp. 27–29.

p. 29, Nobel Prize Winners: Foundation for Biomedical Research, "Nobel Prizes: The Payoff from Animal Research," http://www.fbresearch.org/education/nobels.htm (accessed July 12, 2004).

Chapter 2

pp. 32–35, Greek, C. Ray, M.D., and Jean Swingle Greek, D.V.M., interview with the author, September 30, 2004.

pp. 34–35, Popken, Greg, Ph.D., interview with the author, September 9, 2003.

p. 35, Bennett, interview with the author, September 8, 2003.

p. 39, The Animal Liberation Front http://www.animalliberationfront.com/ALFront/alf_overview.htm (accessed August 28, 2004).

pp. 39–41, PETA, wwww.peta.org/mc/factsheet_display.asp?ID=29 (accessed October 21, 2004).

p. 41, Lisa Lange interview with the author, October 26, 2004.

pp. 41–42, National Animal Interest Alliance, "Animal Rights, Animal Welfare: Which is it?" http://naiaonline.org/body/animal_welfare.htm (accessed August 28, 2004).

pp. 41–42, Woolf, Norma Bennett. National Animal Interest Alliance, "Animal Rights Lawyer Promotes Abolition of Human–Animal Bond," http://naiaonline.org/body/articles/archives/francione.htm (accessed July 12, 2004).

pp. 44–47, Fouts, Roger, with Stephen Tukel Mills, *Next of Kin: What Chimpanzees Have Taught Me About Who We Are* (New York: William Morrow, Inc., 1997), pp. 236, 237, 317, 318.

p. 45, The Gorilla Foundation, http://www.koko.org/world/signlanguage.html (accessed September 1, 2004).

p. 45, http://friendsofwashoe.org/chcichimps/meetthechimps.htm (accessed July 9, 2004).

Chapter 3

pp. 49–51, Black, Harvey. "Monkey Trouble," *The Scientist,* July 28, 2003, http://www.biomedcentral.com/news/20030728/02 (accessed July 12, 2004).

p. 52, Michigan Society for Medical Research http://www.mismr.org/educational/pound.html (accessed September 1, 2004).

pp. 52–53, National Association for Biomedical Research, "Regulation of Biomedical Research Using Animals," 1999 http://www.nabr.org/pdf/green.pdf (accessed July 9, 2004).

p. 52, Foundation for Biomedical Research, "The Pet Theft Myth" http://www.fbresearch.org/education/pet-theft-myth.htm (accessed July 9, 2004).

pp. 53–55. Ahern, Holly. "The Rodent Revolution," *The Scientist,* July 10, 1995.

p. 57, "The Tuskegee Syphilis Experiment," James H. Jones (New York: Free Press, 1993) http://www.infoplease.com/ipa/A0762136.html (accessed August 29, 2004).

pp. 58–59, Greek, C. Ray, M.D., and Jean Swingle Greek, D.V.M., *Specious Science: How Genetics and Evolution Reveal Why Medical Research on Animals Harms Humans* (New York: Continuum, 2002), p. 26.

p. 59, Popken, Greg, review comments.

p. 60, United Network for Organ Sharing, Organ Transplant Waiting List Figures http://www.unos.org (accessed July 12, 2004).

pp. 61–62, Young, John D., V.M.S., M.S., interview with the author, July 24, 2003.

p. 62, USDA Animal Welfare Report Fiscal Year 2002 http://www.aphis.usda.gov/ac/2002ar/ar2002.pdf (accessed July 9, 2004) and National Association for Biomedical Research, "The Humane Care and Treatment of Laboratory Animals" and http://www.nabr.org/pdf/orange.pdf (accessed July 9, 2004).

p. 62, National Association for Biomedical Research, "The Use of Animals in Product Safety Testing," July 26, 2000, p. 2. http://www.nabr.org/pdf/red.pdf (accessed July 9, 2004).

Chapter 4

pp. 65–66, Fano, Alix. *Lethal Laws: Animal Testing, Human Health and Environmental Policy* (New York: Zed Books 1997), p. 14.

p. 66, U.S. Food and Drug Administration, "Animal Testing," http://vm.cfsan.fda.gov/~dms/cos-205.html (accessed July 12, 2004).

pp. 66–67, Food and Drug Administration, History of the FDA http://www.fda.gov/oc/history/historyoffda/longdescriptions/lashlure.html (accessed September 2, 2004).

pp. 67–68, Ibid.

pp. 67–68, Monamy, Vaughn. *Animal Experimentation: A Guide to the Issues* (Cambridge: Cambridge University Press), 2000, pp. 60–61.

p. 70, National Anti-Vivisection Society, "The Draize Test," http://www.navs.org/fact_sheets/fs_draize.cfm?Section_ID=Facts (accessed July 12, 2004).

p. 70, National Association for Biomedical Research, "The Use of Animals in Product Safety Testing," 7-26-00, http://www.nabr.org/pdf/red.pdf (accessed July 9, 2004).

pp. 71–72, Rudacille, Deborah. *The Scalpel and the Butterfly: The Conflict Between Animal Research and Animal Protection* (Berkeley: University of California Press 2000), pp. 298–300.

p. 72, Foundation for Biomedical Research http://www.fbresearch.org/animal-research-faq.htm (accessed July 9, 2004).

Chapter 5

pp. 73–75, Hayhurst, Chris. *Animal Testing: The Animal Rights Debate* (New York: Rosen Publishing Group Inc. 2000), pp. 30–34.

pp. 76–77, "Questions and Answers About the Animal Welfare Act and Its Regulations for Biomedical Research Institutions" http://www.nal.usda.gov/awic/legislat/regsqa.htm (accessed July 12, 2004).

pp. 78–79, Young, John D., D.V.M., M.S., interview with the author, July 24, 2003.

pp. 78–79, 3Rs: Paul, Ellen Frankel, and Jeffrey Paul. *Why Animal Experimentation Matters: The Use of Animals in Medical Research* (New Brunswick, NJ: Transaction Publishers, 2001), pp. 134–135.

pp. 79–80, USDA APHIS Animal Welfare Report, 2002 www.aphis.usda.gov/ac/2002ar/ar2002.pdf (accessed July 9, 2004).

pp. 79–80, Fouts, R. S., Fouts, D. H., and Waters, G. (2002) "The Ethics and Efficacy of Biomedical Research in Chimpanzees With Special Regard to HIV Research" In

A. Fuentes and L. Wolfe (eds.) *Primates Face to Face: Conservation Implications of Human-Nonhuman Primate Interconnections*. Cambridge, United Kingdom: Cambridge University Press), pp. 45–60.

p. 80, Popken, Greg, review comments.

p. 81, Young, John, V.M.S., M.S., interview with the author July 24, 2003.

Chapter 6

pp. 82–84: The Center for Laboratory Animal Welfare, "Animals in the Classroom: A Guide for Elementary and Secondary Educators" http://www.mspca.org/site/pp.asp?c=gtUK40sG&b=126857 (accessed October 22, 2004).

pp. 84–85, National Science Teachers Association, "Guidelines for Responsible Use of Animals in the Classroom," http://www.nsta.org/159&psid=2 (accessed July 6, 2004).

p. 85, Asimov, Isaac. *I, Asimov: A Memoir* (New York, Doubleday & Company, Inc., 1994), p. 90.

pp. 87–88, Klausnitzer, Dorren. "Teachers' Pets Face Expulsion: Groups Raise Health, Cruelty Concerns," *USA Today,* October 3, 2003, p. 20A.

pp. 88–91, Hubbard-Van Stelle, Scott, interview with the author, September 29, 2003.

p. 90, Carlson, Emily. *Wisconsin Week,* "Researchers Learn to Treat Animals Humanely," May 8, 2003 http://www.amprogress.org/news/NewsPrint.cfm?ID=541&c=62 (accessed July 6, 2004).

Chapter 7

pp. 93–94, PETA: http://www.peta.org/about/faq.asp (accessed July 7, 2004).

pp. 93–94, ActivistCash.com www.activistcash.com/organization_blackeye.cfm/oid/21 (accessed August 30, 2004).

pp. 93–94, Foundation for Biomedical Research, "What Opponents Say About Animals and Animal Research" http://www.fbresearch.org/education/opponents.htm (accessed July 9, 2004).

pp. 98–99, Orem, John, interview with the author, October 3, 2003.

pp. 100–101, Paul, Ellen Frankel, and Jeffrey Paul, eds., *Why Animal Experimentation Matters: The Use of*

Animals in Medical Research (New Brunswick & London: Transaction Publishers, 2001), page 60.

Chapter 8

pp. 103–104, Lutherer, Lorenz Otto, and Margaret Sheffield Simon, *Targeted: The Anatomy of an Animal Rights Attack* (Norman, OK: University of Oklahoma Press, 1992), p. 156.

pp. 104–105, Mondics, Chris, "A Harsh Animal-Rights Campaign Targets N.J. Firm, Workers," *The Philadelphia Inquirer,* July 14, 2002 http://www.philly.com/mld/inquirer/3660898.htm? template=contentModules/printstory.jsp (accessed July 6, 2004).

p. 105, Foundation for Biomedical Research, http://www.fbresearch.org/animal-activism/eventsummary.xls\ (accessed July 6, 2004).

pp. 106, http://www.fbresearch.org/animal-activism/violence.htm (accessed July 5, 2004).

pp. 107, http://www.fbresearch.org/journalist/press-releases/061202.htm (accessed June 23, 2004).

p. 108, Animal Enterprise Protection Act http://www.nal.usda.gov/awic/legislat/pl102346.htm (accessed July 7, 2004).

p. 111, Orem, John, interview with the author, October 3, 2003.

p. 111, Popken, Greg, review comments.

Chapter 9

p. 112, National Association for Biomedical Research, "The Use of Animals in Product Safety Testing" http://www.nabr.org/pdf/red.pdf, page 1 (accessed July 6, 2004).

pp. 113–114, Johns Hopkins University Center for Alternatives to Animal Testing http://altweb.jhsph.edu/ (accessed July 13, 2004).

p. 114, Orem, John, interview with the author, October 3, 2003.

p. 114, Bennett, B. Taylor, interview with the author, September 8, 2003.

pp. 117–118, National Institute of Environmental Health Sciences press releases, http://www.niehs.nih.gov/ (accessed September 3, 2004).

pp. 119–120, Greek, Jean Swingle, D.V.M., and C. Ray Greek,

M.D., *What Will We Do if We Don't Experiment On Animals?* (Victoria, Canada: Trafford Publishing 2004), p. 44.

Chapter 10
pp. 122–123, Stevens, Martin, and Andrew Rowan, "An Overview of Animal Testing Issues"
http://www.hsus.org/ace/12508
(accessed September 11, 2004).
p. 123, Popken, Greg, from review comments.
pp. 123–124, Greek, Jean Swingle, D.V.M., and C. Ray Greek, M.D., *What Will We Do If We Don't Experiment on Animals?* pp. 193–198.
pp. 124–126, Humane Society of the United States, "42 Ways to Help Animals in Laboratories"
http://www.hsus.org/ace/13381 (accessed July 13, 2004).

Further Information

Further Reading

Cothran, Helen, *Animal Experimentation: Opposing Viewpoints*. San Diego, CA: Greenhaven Press, 2002.

Hayhurst, Chris, *Animal Testing: The Animal Rights Debate*. New York: The Rosen Publishing Group, Inc., 2000.

Ojeda, Auriana, *The Rights of Animals*. San Diego, CA: Greenhaven Press, 2004.

Woods, Geraldine, *Animal Experimentation and Testing: A Pro/Con Issue*. Berkeley Heights, New Jersey: Enslow Publishers, Inc., 1999.

Web Sites

American Anti-vivisection Society
www.aavs.org

Americans for Medical Progress
www.ampef.org

Animal Owners Unite
www.animalowners.org

Coalition for Medical Progress
www.medicalprogress.org

Foundation for Biomedical Research
www.fbresearch.org

Helping Animals (a PETA-sponsored site)
www.helpinganimals.com

National Animal Interest Alliance
www.naiaonline.org

People for the Ethical Treatment of Animals (PETA)
www.peta.org

Physicians Committee for Responsible Medicine
www.pcrm.org

Bibliography

Blum, Deborah. *The Monkey Wars*. New York: Oxford University Press, 1994.

Fano, Alix. *Lethal Laws: Animal Testing, Human Health and Environmental Policy*. New York: Zed Books, 1997.

Fouts, Roger, with Stephen Mills Tukel. *Next of Kin: What Chimpanzees Have Taught Me About Who We Are*. New York: William Morrow, Inc., 1997.

Greek, C. Ray, M.D., and Jean Swingle Greek, D.V.M. *Sacred Cows and Golden Geese: The Human Cost of Experiments on Animals*. New York: Continuum Publishers, 2000.

————. *Specious Science: How Genetics and Evolution Reveal Why Medical Research on Animals Harms Humans*. New York: Continuum Publishers, 2001.

————*What Will We Do If We Don't Experiment on Animals?* Victoria, Canada: Thofford Publishing, 2004.

Haugen, David M., ed. *At Issue: Animal Experimentation*. San Diego, CA: Greenhaven Press, 2000.

Hayhurst, Chris. *Animal Testing: The Animal Rights Debate.* New York: The Rosen Publishing Group Incorporated, 2000.

Monamy, Vaughan. *Animal Experimentation: A Guide to the Issues.* Cambridge: Cambridge University Press, 2000.

Paul, Ellen Franket, and Jeffrey Paul. *Why Animal Experimentation Matters: The Use of Animals in Medical Research.* New Brunswick, NJ: Transaction Publishers, 2001.

Rudacille, Deborah. *The Scalpel and the Butterfly: The War Between Animal Research and Animal Protection.* New York: Farrar, Straus and Giroux, 2000.

Wise, Stephen M. *Drawing the Line: Science and the Case for Animal Rights.* Cambridge, MA: Perseus Books, 2002.